A Guide to ERISA

Fiduciary Responsibilities

For Advisors and Sponsors of 401(k), 403(b), and Profit Sharing Plans

Charles G. Humphrey, Esq.

A Guide to ERISA Fiduciary Responsibilities

For Advisors and Sponsors of 401(k), 403(b), and Profit Sharing Plans

By

Charles G. Humphrey, Esq.

FPG Publications
Newbury, Massachusetts

A Guide to ERISA Fiduciary Responsibilities

This book contains both original and previously published work. Some material contained herein represents the opinions of the individuals quoted and not necessarily the opinion of the author. In some cases, for metaphorical purposes, this work contains fiction. In such circumstances, names, characters, places, and incidents are either the product of the author's imagination or are used fictitiously. Any resemblance to actual events, locales, or persons, living or dead, is entirely coincidental.

Published by FPG Publications, 28 Green Street, Newbury, Massachusetts 01951

Index by Rachel Lyon, Lyon Publishing Services
(lyonpublishingservices.com)

ISBN-10: 0615958753

ISBN-13: 9780615958750 (FPG Publications)

Library of Congress Control Number: 2014931628
FPG Publications, Newbury, MA

Dedication

For my granddaughters, Zoey Grace and Charlotte (Charley) Rose who are already learning the basic fiduciary principle of putting away their toys, and to my wife, Marcia, who puts up with a lot of my . . . (well, you know) —CGH

Acknowledgments

A "bless you" award goes out to long time colleagues and friends, Henry Smith of the law firm of Smith & Downey, Baltimore, Maryland, and to Phyllis Rimkus of the plan administration firm of Rimkus Marciano & Associates, Rochester, New York. These two, despite their extremely busy schedules, read the manuscript cover to cover and provided me with many useful insights and comments that have greatly improved the book. I am also greatly indebted to Michelle Sullivan and Barbara Danner of the accounting firm of Freed Maxick CPAs, in Buffalo, New York, and veterans of many a plan audit, for their comments on the plan audit section of the book. I acknowledge with deep appreciation the comments, insights, and constructive criticisms of the Fiduciary Plan Governance team and affiliates and in particular Sarah Gormady who helped with organization and formatting, deftly ferreted out typos, errors in grammar and syntax, and challenged me to avoid "lawyer-speak." Thanks also to the wonderful editing team at CreateSpace whose comments and editing smoothed out the final product.

Lastly this book could not have happened without the support and encouragement of Ed Lynch, founder and CEO of Fiduciary Plan Governance, LLC and Neal Dietz of Dietz & Lynch Capital. Thanks Ed and Neal. Alas, despite the very significant contributions mentioned above, I alone bear ultimate responsibility for the contents of this book.

Charles G. Humphrey
Andover, Massachusetts
May 2014

Contents

A Guide to Erisa Fiduciary Responsibilities

What They Are Saying about *A Guide to ERISA Fiduciary Responsibilities*:

"As Fiduciary Plan Governance has developed its industry leading processes for advisors and plan sponsors in meeting ERISA fiduciary responsibilities, Chuck Humphrey has provided us with keen insights and practical knowledge in building them. *A Guide to ERISA Fiduciary Responsibilities* offers Chuck's insights to a much wider audience, clearly and concisely explaining the "how to" of managing fiduciary responsibilities. Plan sponsor committee members, plan advisors, corporate executives, boards of directors, trustees and anyone else even remotely connected to an employer-sponsored retirement plan are well advised to pick up a copy of the book and use it as a valuable day-to-day resource. It is, from my perspective, one of the best tools available to help us all adhere to the "First Rule for Fiduciaries:" which is to "Put Your Interests Last.'" Edward M. Lynch, Jr., Founder and CEO of Fiduciary Plan Governance, Newbury, Massachusetts.

""Fiduciary' is the most dangerous, impactful, misunderstood and misused word in finance. Chuck Humphrey provides clear guidance on the risks and responsibilities for plan sponsors and *A Guide to ERISA Fiduciary Responsibilities* should be mandatory reading for all who administer, oversee, provide or serve on committees for retirement plans. Those who do not seek to understand these risks and responsibilities are at increased risk from the reality of today's fiduciary world." John Hare, Flautt Hare Davis, LLC, Nashville, Tennessee.

A Guide to ERISA Fiduciary Responsibilities is a necessary companion for advisors and plan sponsors that want their 401(k) and 403(b) plans to run cost efficiently and effectively. Written for business people not other experts, it provides how clear, concise guidance how to manage fiduciary responsibilities." Bob Blair, CEO, Retirement Alliance, Manchester New Hampshire.

"*A Guide to ERISA Fiduciary Responsibilities* is essential reading for 401(k) sponsors, executives, boards and those who advise them. Charles Humphrey puts fiduciary principles into practical context, demystifying good fiduciary governance." Kathleen M. McBride, FiduciaryPath, New York, New York.

"I found *A Guide to ERISA Fiduciary Responsibilities* to be a very thorough yet readable guide for anyone who is a fiduciary to a qualified plan. Many people find themselves thrust into the role of a fiduciary with little or no understanding of what their responsibilities and liabilities are, so this is a "must read" for those in that position." Phyllis P. Rimkus, MBA, President, Rimkus, Marciano & Associates, Rochester, New York.

Introduction

A Guide to Fiduciary Responsibility takes a key place in the world of ERISA and the regulation of participant-directed account plans like 401(k) and 403(b) plans.

The world of ERISA and the regulation of participant-directed plans like 401(k)s and 403(b)s became a brew of ambiguities and misconceptions blended in a confusing and contradictory maze of regulations and industry marketing. One could argue that even attempts to improve disclosure and informed decision making have produced a soup of meaningless information and confusion; producing darkness rather than light.

The result is that advisors and particularly plan sponsors act without full knowledge in the important decisions they are making for retirement plans, many believing that all is well and that the retirement of employees is secure.

Chuck Humphrey, an attorney with many years of experience in this area in both government and private practice, introduces clarity and shows how to cut through the maze of laws, regulations and deceptive simplifications to manage plans effectively, reduce costs, and reduce exposure to personal liability for plan fiduciaries.

The challenge for any book in this important area is to convince a sedated public that the principles of defined contribution retirement plans are sound but their current implementation will never deliver the expected results. Squirreling away a portion of your income for the time when the paychecks stop is a fundamentally good idea. But it is only good if a sufficient portion is set aside and never used for other purposes!

The expectation that the miracles of investing will allow $1 saved to become $100 is unrealistic, but has been deliberately promoted by some in the financial community whose first priority is to extract fees with the implied promise of making the miracle happen. This unfortunate state of affairs has occurred in large part because the checks and balances of the system are flawed. At the center of the problem is the fact that employers with little expertise or interest have been assigned the responsibility for the functioning of the entire system. Employers, in their innocence, rely on expert service providers whose own self-interest often trumps the wellbeing of the plan.

This book addresses these problems by providing plan sponsors and their advisors with the tools they need to protect plan interests, expose misleading representations, and put themselves on an even footing with those selling products and services.

Louis S. Harvey, President & CEO, Dalbar
Boston, Massachusetts

Why This Book?

With my thirty-five-plus years of experience in the employee-benefits field, it does not surprise me when I hear a business owner say, "We have people who take care of that," when referring to his or her company's 401(k) plan. In fact, many employers do have people who take care of things: TPAs, accountants, brokers, agents, consultants, and attorneys. This is good. But by making that comment, business owners (or for that matter tax-exempt entity executives when they are refer to their 403(b) plans) reveal a misunderstanding of a key aspect of plan sponsorship. When one of the people who takes care of things makes a mistake, the company, or someone at the company, is exposed to liability. The business owners, in fact, are responsible—not the provider. This is due to the complicated maze of fiduciary liability under the federal law known as ERISA. Advisors and plan sponsors who have command of this essential fact are already a step ahead.

Many books have been written about ERISA fiduciary responsibility but none have attempted to cover the topic comprehensively in language that business people understand and many provide endless lists of rules with no instruction on how the rules might be complied with. This book takes aim at that void by speaking non-technically and by showing plan sponsors and advisors how to manage their obligations under the rules.

ERISA's fiduciary standards are "the highest known to the law."[1] Further, as has often been repeated, a "pure heart" and an "empty head" are not enough to avoid liability as an ERISA fiduciary.[2] If they are to have any chance at compliance, plan sponsors must know who is a fiduciary, what plans are subject to ERISA, and what fiduciary obligations ERISA imposes.

If a plan sponsor can get stuck with liability because of the actions of others, doesn't it make sense for it to know something about the plan and the providers servicing it? An employer that employs drivers will qualify the drivers for the job and monitor their performance because employing a driver without a license or who has a health or substance problem could cost the employer a lot of money. It makes good business sense to take precautions. It's no different for a 401(k) or

[1] Donovan v. Bierwirth, 680 F.2d 263, 272 (2d Cir. 1982).

[2] Defelice v. US Airways, 497 F.3d 410 (4th Circ. 2007).

403(b) plan sponsor. The sponsor needs to know whether plan service providers are capable of doing the job, what they are doing, and whether they are worth what the plan is paying them.

The very real sticking point for the plan sponsor is figuring out what, in practice, needs to be done. This is not easy because 401(k) and 403(b) plans are burdened with complicated fee arrangements involving various types of indirect compensation, asymmetrical relationships in which the providers know more than the sponsor, and complicated rules imposed by the federal agencies with authority over these plans. Plan sponsors have limited capacity to deal with this complexity. An advisor who is cognizant of these rules can provide significant value in helping a plan sponsor survive and perhaps thrive under them.

While some in the government might think so, managing a plan does not come before running the business. But plan sponsors have to do something. Their liability is not going away simply because they have a business to run. No one will accept the argument that "I had lots of other things to do," including employees (and their attorneys), government agencies, and the courts. Employers have a *plan* to run, too. The surprising thing is that plan sponsors can manage their plans and their plans' providers without sacrificing their core mission of running the business. Doing so involves organizing plan oversight in critical areas and seeking expert help when a matter cannot be handled "in-house."

Good fiduciary governance requires an ongoing commitment to process and procedure, or what some have called "procedural prudence." It requires keeping abreast of the latest regulatory and retirement industry developments and overseeing service providers to ensure that they are capable of and are performing their plan obligations for a reasonable fee.

As mentioned earlier, the aim of this book is to show plans sponsors, their executives and boards, and their advisors how to manage a plan effectively, efficiently, and economically. I trust this book will give advisors, plan-sponsor decision makers and fiduciaries real and useful insights into the how–to of plan management and fiduciary responsibility and that it will be a resource for common sense information on how to run a plan.

Finally, this book is not intended to be a treatise on employee-benefits law. For that there are many excellent volumes available. Nor is the book intended to provide legal advice. For that there are many excellent employee-benefits attorneys.

How to Read the Book

This book is intended to provide information, as its subtitle indicates, to advisors to and sponsors of 401(k), 403(b) and profit sharing plans. Yet the reader will not see one reference in the text to profit sharing plans. This is intended, as the use of the term would have added many additional words and made unnecessarily complex and confusing sentences. So, unless the context clearly indicates otherwise references to "401(k) plans" and "plans" should be read as also referring to "profit sharing plans."

The 403(b) plans described in this book generally are the ones subject to the jurisdiction and enforcement authority of the United States Department of Labor. They come under that authority because the level of plan sponsor involvement is significant enough to make this so. For example, a plan sponsor merely offering payroll slots for multiple vendors is not subject to the federal law fiduciary rules described in this book. On the other hand more active involvement such as promotion of the plan, selection and monitoring plan investments or the making of plan sponsor contributions put the plan within the jurisdiction of the Labor Department as an ERISA plan. The 403(b) ERISA plans referred to in the book are referred to as "403(b) plans."

Most, but not all of the rules described in the book, apply to all plans but some do not apply to 403(b) plans. When these rules differ for 403(b) plans it is pointed out.

The term "plan sponsor" or "sponsor" is frequently used and always refers to the company or employer of employees that are covered under the plan. It is sometimes used interchangeably with "fiduciary" especially when referring to plan sponsors acting in the capacity of plan administrator, which they often do. It must be remembered though that a plan sponsor is not always a plan administrator.

Where the word "Code" appears in the book it always refers to the "Internal Revenue Code. And "ERISA" is the Employee Retirement Income Security Act, the legal bedrock on which the things discussed in this book are based.

The U.S. Department of Labor is referred to throughout the book as "Labor Department.

Finally, many of the principles described are of general applicability to other types of benefit plans such as defined benefit plans, money purchase plans, and welfare benefit plans. Although the reader did not purchase the book with these types of plans in mind, these principles offer a basic structure for the fiduciary management of these plans too.

CHAPTER 1

Who Has Fiduciary Responsibility for Your Plan?

For plan sponsors and their advisors, one of the most confusing aspects of maintaining a 401(k) or 403(b) plan is identifying who has fiduciary responsibility for it. Confusing pitches from vendors, service-agreement legalese and fine print, and lengthy and "unreadable" plan documents do not make comprehension any easier. Terms such as "fiduciary" and "service provider" are commonly used in the industry but are not commonly understood by plan sponsors or their plans' providers. Plans may involve multiple vendors, each one responsible for different (but often very limited) aspects of the plan's administration and investments. Many vendors will claim that they are "taking care of it" for the sponsor or that "we've got your back." For the plan sponsor, understanding where its responsibilities end and the service provider's begin is a critical task. What those responsibilities are is a very real but necessary challenge if they are to protect their own interests and the interests of participants. The plan sponsor must ask not only "Who's on first?" but also "What is that person doing on first?"

A. Fiduciaries Assigned by Plan Provisions

Every plan must assign fiduciary responsibility to one or more "named fiduciaries that will have responsibility for managing and operating the plan."[3] This person

[3] ERISA Sec. 402(a)(1).

or entity[4] is either directly named or appointed under a procedure set forth in the plan.[5] The purpose of requiring a named fiduciary is to determine responsibility for any mismanagement of the plan.[6]

Larger plan sponsors will often assign this responsibility to a plan committee that controls the operation and administration of the plan. A plan provision might specify one or more persons by name or title that will sit on the committee. This responsibility might also be assigned to an individual or a position, such as the vice president of human resources or the chief financial officer. Failure to designate fiduciary responsibility is likely to result in the plan sponsor or even its board of directors being held responsible for the plan's operation. For smaller plan sponsors conducting business as, for example, sole proprietorships, this responsibility will most likely reside with the owner, unless the plan provides for alternative assignments of the responsibility.

Pointer: Because most plan sponsors rely on standardized prototype or IRS preapproved-documentation, plan sponsors should scrutinize the provisions dealing with fiduciary allocation of authority to ascertain where this responsibility is assigned.

B. Plan Administrator

The plan administrator is normally an individual or entity that is a fiduciary to the plan and is designated in the plan document as such. If the plan document does not say who the plan administrator is, the plan administrator is the plan sponsor.[7]

Pointer: Smart plan draftsmanship will make clear when committees or individuals are appointed plan administrator that they act on behalf of the plan sponsor.

A person is a fiduciary if he or she has discretionary authority or responsibility for the administration of the plan and has a duty to act under the rules set forth in ERISA for fiduciary conduct. On the other hand, a person who does not have discretionary authority or responsibility for the plan's administration and performs purely ministerial[8] tasks is not a plan fiduciary and is not bound by fiduciary requirements.

---

[4] Fiduciaries may be individuals, partnerships, joint ventures, corporations, mutual companies, joint-stock companies, trusts, estates, unincorporated associations, or employee organizations. ERISA Sec. 3(9).

[5] ERISA Sec. 402(a)(2).

[6] H.R. Conf. Rep. No. 93-1280, 93d Cong., 2d Sess. (1974) (ERISA Conference Report).

[7] ERISA Sec. 3(16)(A).

[8] "Ministerial" is defined in Merriam Webster on-line dictionary, as visited on February 22, 2014 as "relating to or being an act done after ascertaining the existence of a

Examples of ministerial acts or clerical functions that do not give rise to fiduciary status include the following:

- Applying rules for determining eligibility for participation or benefits
- Calculating services and compensation credits for benefits
- Preparing employee communications material
- Maintaining participants' service and employment records
- Preparing reports required by government agencies
- Calculating benefits
- Orienting new participants and advising participants of their rights and options under the plan
- Collecting contributions and applying contributions as provided in the plan
- Preparing reports concerning participants' benefits
- Making recommendations to others for decisions with respect to plan administration[9]

Pointer: Plan sponsors often misunderstand the nature of the services provided by third-party administrators (TPAs) and as a consequence may assume that TPAs are fiduciaries when in fact they are not. Under typical TPA arrangements and agreements, TPAs do not interpret plan provisions but merely follow them and are therefore not fiduciaries. Plan sponsors should understand that fiduciary responsibility (and liability) for plan administration resides in them or the named fiduciary designated as plan administrator—not the TPA. Interestingly, a new type of service provider, the so-called section 3(16) administrator, has emerged in recent years that, under agreement with the plan sponsor, assumes much of the sponsor's ERISA responsibilities. These services and other arrangements are discussed in chapter 16.

C. Other Fiduciaries as Defined by ERISA

ERISA makes certain other persons fiduciaries by definition, regardless of plan provisions or formal designations. Status as a fiduciary may be determined by a person's functions with respect to a plan and does not depend on a formal undertaking or agreement.

---

specified state of facts in obedience to a legal order *without exercise of personal judgment or discretion*" (Emphasis added). See http://www.merriam-webster.com/dictionary/ministerial.

[9] Labor Department Reg. Sec. 2509-75-8, D-2.

ERISA defines a fiduciary as any person or entity that:

1. Exercises any discretionary control or authority over plan assets
2. Exercises any discretionary authority or control respecting management and the disposition of assets
3. Renders investment advice for a fee or other compensation, direct or indirect, with respect to any moneys or other property of the plan, or has any authority or responsibility to do so
4. Has any discretionary authority or control with respect to the administration of the plan[10]

In other words, people or entities can become fiduciaries even if a plan document does not designate them or no one formally appoints them as such. For example, a TPA that exercised the power to write checks on a plan account and wrote checks to itself to pay its own fees was found to be a fiduciary because it exercised discretionary control over plan assets.[11] The trite summary of this principal is, "If you walk like a fiduciary, talk like a fiduciary, and look like a fiduciary, you are a fiduciary."

Pointer: This type of fiduciary can be created within a plan sponsor's organization often without realizing it is happening. For example, when the person in HR who is assigned calculation of benefits goes beyond the mere calculation and interprets an ambiguous plan provision, the employee may be surprised to learn that he or she has made him or herself a fiduciary by those actions, and the plan sponsor may be surprised to know it has lost control of the processes. For these reasons, plan sponsors must clearly articulate roles for those involved with the plan.

Trustees are likely to be fiduciaries under the ERISA definition simply because of the nature of the services they provide. However, when plan agreements do "not accord the trustees any discretionary authority over investment decisions," they may not be considered fiduciaries.[12] The latter might occur when an institutional trustee has no investment discretion and is hired solely to hold assets in a custodial capacity and to take investment directions from a plan committee or an investment manager.

An *investment manager* is a fiduciary. This is a person or entity other than a named or other trustee that has the authority to manage, acquire, and dispose of plan assets and will be either a registered investment adviser under the

[10] ERISA Secs. 3(21)(A) and 3(9).

[11] Briscoe v. Fine, 2006 U.S. App. LEXIS 9208 (6th Cir. 2006).

[12] Arakelian v. National W. Life Ins. Co., 748 F. Supp. 17 (D.D.C.1990).

Investment Advisers Act of 1940, a bank as defined in that act, or an insurance company with the power to manage, acquire, or dispose of any plan asset under the laws of more than one state. If the investment manager acknowledges, in writing, to the appointing fiduciary that it is a fiduciary with respect to the plan, the appointing fiduciary will be relieved of liability for the investment manager's individual investment decisions. However, the appointing fiduciary (e.g., plan committee, board, or plan administrator) will *not* ever be relieved of liability for its initial appointment and subsequent monitoring of the manager's performance.[13]

To put it another way, if the investment manager fouls up, the appointing fiduciary is not liable for that foul-up. But if the investment manager engages in a persistent pattern of poor performance, misfeasance, or malfeasance that the appointing fiduciary fails to detect because it is not overseeing the investment manager, liability has arrived at the appointing fiduciary's doorstep.

Those who provide investment advice are fiduciaries, sometimes called *investment-advice fiduciaries*. An investment-advice fiduciary is someone other than a trustee or investment manager who passes this five-prong test set forth in Labor Department regulations. Investment-advice fiduciaries:

1. make recommendations on investing in, purchasing or selling securities or other property;
2. on a regular basis;
3. pursuant to a mutual understanding that the advice will:
4. serve as a primary basis for investment decisions; and
5. be individualized to the particular needs of the plan.

Investment advice is not considered advice from a fiduciary unless *all* five elements are satisfied.

Pointer: The plan sponsor must ask the service provider to tell it in writing whether it is an ERISA fiduciary. The five-prong test is very hard to satisfy. In fact, many brokerage firms set up their relationships with plan sponsors to make sure they are *not* fiduciaries under this test. This means that in providing advice to plan sponsors, they are under no obligation to act in the best interests of the plan. In fact, the broker may offer an investment fund to the plan sponsor that is in a more expensive share class so the broker can make more money from the relationship without violating ERISA or any applicable securities law. Many who present themselves as providing disinterested investment advice are not in fact doing that.

---

[13] ERISA Secs. 3(38) and 402(c)(3).

Pointer: Once the plan sponsor has determined that the service provider is a fiduciary it must consider carefully the nature of the fiduciary obligation as stated in the service provider's agreements. Does the plan sponsor understand that the promise is limited to the provision of investment advice and that the adviser does not make investment decisions for the plan? If the plan sponsor wants to place investment decision making in another, it should be talking with someone who is willing to assume that responsibility under an investment management agreement.

D. Those Who Are Not Fiduciaries

In general, professionals such as attorneys, accountants, and actuaries are not fiduciaries simply because they render services on behalf of a plan. They may become fiduciaries if they exercise decision-making authority that goes beyond the influence they have as professionals.[14]

Officers, members of the board of directors, and employees are not fiduciaries simply by reason of holding their positions.[15] They are fiduciaries if they have any of the four responsibilities listed in the second paragraph of section C, above. For example, a CEO who does not sit on a plan committee and has no involvement with the plan is not a fiduciary; one that does is.

Mutual-fund companies and their advisers are not fiduciaries, even though they obviously have investment discretion over the investments in the funds. Nor are *insurance companies* fiduciaries, although certain circumstances may make them so. For example, an insurance company may become a fiduciary when it retains authority to amend terms of the annuity contract without the consent of plan trustees.[16]

Broker-dealers are generally not fiduciaries,[17] although the industry does much to confuse the issue, leading many plan sponsors to believe that this relationship is fiduciary in nature. This is important to understand because so many plan arrangements are set up through brokers. Brokers operate under a *lesser* suitability

---

[14] Pappas v. Buck Consultants, Inc., 923 F.2d 531 (7th Cir. 1991).

[15] Labor Department Reg. Sec. 2509.75-8, D-4, D-5.

[16] Associates in Adolescent Psychiatry v. Home Life Insurance Co., 941 F2d. 561 (7th Cir. 1991), cert. denied, 502 U.S. 1099 (1992).

[17] Broker-dealers are not considered fiduciaries merely because they execute securities transactions and meet certain other requirements set forth in Labor Dep. Reg. Sec. 2510.321(d)(1).

standard that allows them to act in their own self-interest, while fiduciaries do not and must act exclusively for the benefit of the plan.[18]

Insurance companies are generally not fiduciaries although if they manage an insurance company separate account on behalf of a plan would be fiduciaries.

Fiduciaries are not subject to fiduciary liability for plan matters they have not been assigned responsibility for. For example, a trustee that holds plan assets does not have liability for the investment of any plan assets that are separately managed and invested by a third-party investment manager. Liability may emerge for such a fiduciary under the "co-fiduciary" rules if the fiduciary acquires knowledge of another fiduciary's misfeasance and fails to act. This aspect of fiduciary liability is discussed in chapter 2.

E. Distinction between Settlor and Fiduciary Activities

Plan sponsors and their officers are in two separate, distinct—and sometimes conflicting roles. This is tolerated up to a point under the ERISA sanctioned "two hat" doctrine. In other words, a plan sponsor officer is allowed to sit on a plan committee as a fiduciary and to make decisions on behalf of the plan. However, if a plan decision comes up that brings officer's interests as an employee of the plan sponsor into direct conflict with his or her obligations to the plan, that individual must step aside in favor of a neutral party or find another way to resolve the conflict. This situation might arise when plan sponsor contributions are delinquent or when in a decision sell or hold plan sponsor stock is required.

Decisions relating to the design, establishment, and termination of the plan are *settlor* functions, which are not subject to ERISA fiduciary provisions. Thus, a plan sponsor's decision to terminate a plan need not take into account the interests of the participants. That decision is of a business nature clearly outside the purview of ERISA.[19] On the other hand, actions taken by a plan sponsor in appointing fiduciaries or contracting with other service providers are *fiduciary* in nature and subject to ERISA's fiduciary responsibility provisions.[20] For example,

[18] For more on this, read our colleague Mark Mensack's pieces on this topic, including "The Moral Hazard of Too Big to Jail," *Journal of Compensation and Benefits*, May/June 2013; "The Moral Hazard of Uninformed Consent," *Journal of Compensation and Benefits*, March/April 2013; and "The Wizard of Oz, Retirement Plans, and You," *Journal of Compensation and Benefits*, November/December 2012.

[19] Conversely, expenses incurred up to the decision to terminate a plan may not be paid out of plan assets because they do not relate to an activity of the plan or to its administration.

[20] Expenses related to these functions may be paid from plan assets as a cost of the administration of the plan.

communications to employees regarding plan benefits and features have been held to be fiduciary in nature.[21]

Pointer: Lines may blur with respect to some matters. For example, the holding of plan sponsor stock in a plan raises very real conflict issues requiring the appointment of an independent fiduciary responsible for decision-making regarding the holding of the stock. It is important for plan sponsors to adopt procedures that identify and address conflicts not allowed under the two-hat doctrine.

F. Potential Impact of Proposed Regulations on Investment-Advice Fiduciaries

In October 2010 the Labor Department issued proposed regulations[22] that would substantially change the definition of an investment-advice fiduciary, bringing many providers not currently fiduciaries under a new definition replacing the five-prong test described in section C above. The proposed regulations would eliminate the requirements that investment advice be provided on a regular basis and serve as the primary basis for investment decisions. The department withdrew the proposed regulations mostly because of opposition from the financial services industry and has announced it will re-propose the regulations. As of this writing, the re-proposed regulations have not been issued.

Pointer: Plan fiduciaries should watch for the re-proposal of these regulations because if they are finalized as originally proposed, many existing relations, in particular brokerage-plan ones, will have to be substantially reordered.

G. Those Who Cannot Be Fiduciaries

Persons convicted of certain crimes are barred from serving as plan fiduciaries.[23] These crimes include robbery, bribery, extortion, grand larceny, embezzlement, fraud, grand larceny, burglary, arson, murder, rape, kidnapping, perjury, and assault with intent to kill—though this is not the complete list.

Pointer: When qualifying a candidate for a fiduciary position, inquiry should be made about the person's past in this regard. Prudence may indicate the necessity of a criminal background check.

---

[21] Varity Corp. v. Howe, 514 U.S. 1082 (1996).

[22] Proposed Labor Dept. Reg. Sec. 2520.3-21(c)(l)((i)(a)(A)(1) to (3).

[23] ERISA Sec. 411.

H. Fiduciary Delegation

Delegation aims to allocate responsibility and associated liabilities to those with the capacity to handle the responsibility. In delegating fiduciary responsibility, a fiduciary must be aware of this important consideration: although plan fiduciaries can delegate responsibility, they cannot abdicate their responsibilities. By delegating fiduciary responsibility, a fiduciary cannot rid itself of liability entirely. Delegating fiduciaries have liability for the delegation decision and for ongoing monitoring of the persons or entities to which responsibilities have been delegated. Documentation of the delegation is critical to limiting fiduciary liability.

CHAPTER 2

What Is Fiduciary Responsibility?

Fiduciary responsibility should not be hard to understand but it seems so when expressed in the abstract and in the terms of the law itself. The concept comes at advisers and plan sponsors almost as a language from another planet --- a foreign tongue. It is at once a yardstick against which behavior is measured and a to-do list. The problem is ERISA does not tell plan sponsors how to do it. This chapter discusses the high standard against which fiduciary conduct is measured and describes how it is done.

A. ERISA Standard of Conduct

ERISA fiduciaries are subject to standards of conduct that derive from common the law in the general terms and as specifically set forth in the statute. A fiduciary must discharge his or her duties:

- solely in the interests of plan participants and beneficiaries and for the exclusive purpose of providing benefits;
- with the care, skill, prudence, and diligence of a prudent person acting in like capacity with like aims;
- by diversifying investments; and
- in accordance with plan documents.[24]

[24] ERISA Sec. 404.

Pointer: The phrase "prudent man" is used above but the phrase to remember and one used throughout this book is "prudent expert." This is the level of expertise, experience, and knowledge that all fiduciary conduct is measured against.

In addition, plan fiduciaries must take care to avoid prohibited transactions involving the plan and interested parties or disqualified persons.[25] For example, if a plan purchases real estate from the plan sponsor, it has engaged in a prohibited transaction with the sponsor that is subject to excise taxes and other significant legal consequences.[26] The statutory underpinning of this prohibition is that the plan sponsor, by virtue of its relationship to the plan, is in a position to take advantage of the plan for its own benefit.

The rules are intended to protect plan interests and the dissipation of plan assets to interested parties who, in the absence of the rules, might advantage themselves to the detriment of the plan.

B. Principal Areas of Responsibility

The general rules of fiduciary conduct do not give plan sponsors a guide as to what they must do as fiduciaries. It is clear that the standard of conduct is high, but for what are plan sponsors responsible?

There are five key areas of responsibility, each of which will be discussed in more detail later in this book and each of which must be accounted for on at least an annual basis. They include responsibility for:

1. **Plan documentation**. This includes maintenance of plan documents in compliance with Internal Revenue Code requirements.
2. **Plan administration**. This involves running the plan, from eligibility and vesting determinations to allocation of contributions and distributions. Employee communications, including required notices, and tax reporting to the IRS are also important parts of administration.
3. **Plan investments**. For most 401(k) plans and all 403(b) plans, this means establishing a lineup of investment options for participants who direct their own investments.[27]
4. **Selection and oversight of plan service providers**. This is arguably one of the most important responsibilities plan sponsors and their internal

[25] ERISA Secs.404 and 406, and corresponding provisions of Internal Revenue Code Sec. 4975.

[26] ERISA Sec. 406; Code Sec. 4975.

[27] There is no legal requirement to allow participants to direct investment in their own accounts. In practice though, over the years this has become the dominant form of investment in 401(k) plans.

fiduciaries have. Excess costs and substandard services can adversely and significantly affect plan performance and employee retirement savings.

5. **Reporting to the government (Form 5500 series).** This is an informational report that plan sponsors (plan administrators) must file every year with the Labor Department under penalty of perjury. Both the Labor Department and the IRS use the information provided on the form as an important source for developing their respective investigations and examinations.

A sixth very important area of responsibility, although arguably not at this point a fiduciary responsibility under ERISA, is the **determination of plan effectiveness**. This involves establishing whether the plan achieves retirement-savings goals for its participants, ensuring that employees are provided with investment education, calculating whether savings rates on an individual basis are sufficient, and measuring the appropriateness of investment allocations for achieving individual retirement goals.

Pointer: Efficient management of these areas consistent with general fiduciary obligations requires the creation of a governance structure whose central element is accountability. Each of these responsibilities should be put on the plan sponsor's calendar every year and reviewed. Any problem discovered during this process must be appropriately addressed. Each plan sponsor decides on its own approach to fiduciary governance based on its size, resources, and corporate structure.

C. Delegating Fiduciary Authority and Why Delegation Doesn't Make Fiduciary Liability Go Away Entirely

When a board of directors or named fiduciary appoints someone to perform a fiduciary (or a non-fiduciary) function, it commits itself to: (1) making a prudent decision about the selection of that person[28] and (2) monitoring the performance of that person. The appointing fiduciary will be liable both for the initial appointment and for any failure to monitor performance.

Pointer: Many boards and committees do not understand this responsibility and do not take appropriate steps to monitor those appointed. The best approach is to require periodic reporting from them. For example, it is a best practice for a board in the exercise of its oversight responsibilities to require an annual written

[28] That is, the service is necessary to the operation of the plan, the fees paid for the service are reasonable, and the fiduciary believes after a due diligence process that the appointee can provide the services promised in a satisfactory manner.

report from a plan committee. No board would want to be in the position of the board of directors of Agway, Inc., whose members were barred from service to that company's employee-benefit plans unless they completed a fiduciary training course and which was required to restore almost $9 million to the plan and pay nearly $900,000 in civil penalties.[29] All because they failed to give the Agway plan proper attention.

D. Responsibility for the Actions of Other Fiduciaries

Fiduciaries are generally liable for responsibilities that are within their purview, either pursuant to an agreement—with, for example, a financial institution trustee—or as specified in plan documents. However, this does not mean that these fiduciaries are off the hook for the actions of other fiduciaries with different responsibilities.

A fiduciary may be responsible for the breach of another plan fiduciary in each of the following circumstances if the fiduciary:

- Participates knowingly in, or knowingly undertakes to conceal, an act or omission of another fiduciary, knowing that the breach of a fiduciary is a fiduciary breach
- By failure to comply with the requirement to discharge his or her duties solely in the interests of plan participants and beneficiaries, enables another fiduciary to commit a breach
- Has knowledge of a breach by another fiduciary and fails to make reasonable efforts under the circumstances to remedy the breach[30]

This liability may attach to successor fiduciaries if the successor knows of the breach of a predecessor and fails to take whatever steps are necessary to remedy the breach.[31]

Pointer: When taking over a plan from a previous fiduciary, the new fiduciary should attempt to get a good sense that the previous fiduciary's records are in order and that at the surface level, there are no irregularities that might call for further investigation.

---

[29] "US Labor Department Recovers $8.6 Million for Workers in Settlement Involving Agway 401(k) Plan in New York," US Department of Labor Release Number 08-1529-NEW, October 23, 2008, accessed August 24, 2013,www.dol.gov/ebsa/newsroom/08-1529-NEW.html.

[30] ERISA Sec. 405(a).

[31] Labor Department Advisory Opinion Letter 76-95.

E. When Regular Plan Fiduciaries Do Not Have Needed Expertise

Because fiduciary conduct is measured against the standard of an expert familiar with plan matters, plan-sponsor fiduciaries that do not have the expertise to address a plan decision must seek that expertise from one that does. Often this expertise will be sought in the case of truly singular plan events such as the hiring of an "independent fiduciary" as a condition of a Labor Department grant of an individual prohibited transaction exemption (discussed in chapter 3). Much more often this expertise will be sought under more prosaic circumstances such as in the hiring of plan service providers when it is sensible and necessary to put the evaluation of their fees and services in the hands of an industry expert.

CHAPTER 3

What Are Fiduciary Liabilities under ERISA?

One cannot hear the word "fiduciary" today without hearing its partner, the word "liability." Like Katharine Hepburn and Spencer Tracy they are linked eternally. Liability or more specifically exposure to it is a significant part of what it means to be a fiduciary. This chapter discusses the various ways fiduciary liability may arise.

A. Claims for Fiduciary Breach

Errors or omissions in fiduciary or co-fiduciary responsibilities can lead to liability. The Labor Department, a participant, a beneficiary, or another fiduciary may bring claims for appropriate relief.[32] Many of these claims are brought for recovery of monetary losses due to a fiduciary breach, though a breach need not have resulted in a loss to the plan.

Some suits seek to enjoin prohibited practices or to obtain equitable relief. Equitable relief provides the courts with the flexibility to craft a wide range of remedies.

One example is the retroactive reinstatement of employees as participants to permit restitution of benefits.[33] Restitution of plan losses or the disgorgement of profits used as a result of the breach would be an appropriate equitable relief

---

[32] ERISA Secs. 409 and 502(a).

[33] Varity v. Howe, 116 S. Ct. 1065 (1996).

remedy. The goal of restitution is to put the plan in the position it would have been in had the breach not occurred, which is sometimes called "making the plan whole."

In another case the Labor Department obtained a permanent injunction barring an investment adviser from acting in a fiduciary or any other kind of service capacity with respect to any employee-benefit plans.[34]

Claims of fiduciary breach are personal in nature, meaning a fiduciary's personal assets can be reached, so a fiduciary's house, bank accounts, stock holdings, and personal property can be lost. Fiduciaries who breach their fiduciary duties, responsibilities, or obligations are personally liable to make good to the plan the losses resulting from the breach and to restore to the plan any profits they made using its assets. A fiduciary is also liable for any equitable or remedial relief that the court may deem appropriate, including removal of the fiduciary. A court may award attorney's fees and costs to the side that wins.

Corporate officers acting in a fiduciary capacity do not have the protection of a corporate shield. Personal liability should be a critical consideration when plan sponsors are making—and officers are considering accepting—a fiduciary appointment. Plan fiduciaries involved in the selection of plan service providers should be especially concerned given the spate of cases against fiduciaries for payment of excess fees to these providers.[35]

B. ERISA 502(l) 20 Percent Penalty

The Labor Department also can impose a civil penalty under ERISA section 502(1) for any breach of fiduciary responsibility or knowing participation in such breach by any other person. The penalty is equal to 20 percent of the "applicable recovery amount," which is the amount the department recovers under any settlement agreement with it, any court order, or any action instituted by the department. The Labor Department, in its discretion, can waive the penalty if it determines severe financial hardship would result or the fiduciary acted in good faith.

POINTER: This penalty can often be avoided with deft legal representation by coming to a mutual understanding with the Labor Department that is short of an actual settlement. Retaining competent ERISA counsel is critical to a successful result.

---

[34] Beck v. Levering, 947 F.2d 639 (2d Cir. 1991).

[35] For example, see Tussey v. ABB, Inc., et al, No. 2:06-CV-04305-NKL, 2012 WL 111329, where the plan fiduciaries (1) failed to follow the plan's investment policy statement, (2) selected high-cost investments, (3) failed to monitor and renegotiate record-keeping revenue, and (4) replaced low-fee funds with high-fee funds.

C. Prohibited Transaction Sanctions

Chapter 2 explains that plan fiduciaries are subject to a general standard of conduct whose main elements are the duty of exclusive loyalty to the plan and professional competence. These general duties are supplemented in the ERISA statutory scheme by *prohibition of specific activities* between plans and persons defined as disqualified persons and parties in interest.[36]

As one court explained, the prohibited transactions rules are an attempt by Congress to prevent transactions with a high potential for loss or insider abuse.[37] For example, making a loan to the plan sponsor or purchasing real estate owned by the plan sponsor or other parties in interest[38] is prohibited because of this high potential for abuse.

For some years now, the Labor Department has focused on plan sponsor failures to deliver salary-deferral contributions to their plans on a timely basis. More recently, the Labor Department, through regulatory rule, defined as a prohibited transaction the failure of plan service providers to provide fee and services information to plans. The Labor Department found that without the provision of this information, plans had been disadvantaged in dealing with more sophisticated service providers.[39] These rules are discussed in chapter 7.

Individuals or entities defined as disqualified persons or parties in interest include the following:

- The plan's sponsor, some of its owners (and related companies), and officers
- The plan's fiduciaries
- The plan's service providers

The transactions that are prohibited are:

- Furnishing goods, services, or facilities
- Selling, exchanging, or leasing property
- Lending money or otherwise extending credit
- Transferring the benefit plan income or assets to or allowing their use by or for a disqualified person or party in interest

---

[36] ERISA Sec. 406, and corresponding provisions of Code Sec. 4975.

[37] Cutaiar v. Marshall, 590 F.2d 523 (3rd Cir. 1979).

[38] Parties in interest are defined as "disqualified persons" under the corresponding provisions of the Internal Revenue Code.

[39] See Labor Department fact sheet titled "Final Regulation Relating to Service Provider Disclosures Under Section 408(b)(2)," Labor Department website, accessed August 24, 2013, http://www.dol.gov/ebsa/newsroom/fs408b2finalreg.html#.UKTWmKUZeJU.

- Acts by a disqualified person who is a fiduciary that involve dealing with the income or assets of the plan for that person's own benefit

Pointer: The "use by" prohibition comes up frequently with smaller plan sponsors that want to use their plans to purchase vacation property and then, of course, would like to vacation there. The purchase of the property is not a problem, assuming it makes investment sense and the purchase is not from a party in interest or disqualified person. But the use of the property by the owner is a prohibited transaction.

Fiduciaries are, in addition, prohibited from doing the following:

- Acquiring and holding certain plan sponsor securities and real property[40]
- Acting in a transaction involving the plan on behalf of a party whose interests are adverse to the interests of the plan or its participants and beneficiaries
- Receiving consideration for their own personal account from parties dealing with the plan in connection with transactions involving the plan [41]

Exemptions are made for transactions either expressly in the statute for specific transactions (statutory exemptions) or under the Labor Department's authority to grant upon request or on its own motion administrative exemptions.

A partial list of **statutory exemptions** includes the following:

- Participant loans
- Contracting or making reasonable arrangements with parties in interest for goods and services to establish or operate the plan
- Transactions in connection with providing participants investment advice
- Receipt by a fiduciary of reasonable compensation for services rendered or for the reimbursement of expenses properly and actually incurred in the performance of duties for the plan—*except* that any employee who already receives full-time pay from the employer/sponsor is not entitled to compensation
- Acquisition of, and holding of "qualifying real property" and "qualifying employer securities."

The Labor Department may grant administrative exemptions to individual applicants on a case-by-case basis (**individual exemptions**) or for classes of

[40] ERISA Sec. 406(a).

[41] ERISA Sec. 406(b).

transactions pursuant to the department's own initiative and authority (**class exemptions**). As the name implies class exemptions are available to plans that can fit their transactions within the terms and conditions of the exemption and without an individual filing or application to the Labor Department.

Individual exemptions have been granted in the following representative areas:

- In acquisitions and mergers
- For asset allocation advice/investment allocation advice
- Assignment by plans of rights, claims, and causes of action
- For cross-trading
- Purchases of customer notes by a plan (notes acquired by the plan sponsor in the ordinary course of business)
- For hedge fund investments
- Holding of employer securities
- In-kind (property) contributions to a plan
- Purchases and leases of real property between a plan and party in interest
- Loans
- Provision of services
- Investments in venture capital funds

Class exemptions have been granted by the Labor Department in the following representative areas:

- Bank collective funds
- Transactions between plans and broker-dealers, reporting dealers, and banks
- Sharing and leasing office space and administrative services and goods with respect to a multiple-employer plan
- Insurance agents and brokers
- Lending of securities by plans to broker-dealers
- Transactions authorized or required by a court order or court-approved settlement
- Receipt of certain financial services in connection with the establishment of an IRA, Keogh, or SEP
- A plan's or fiduciary's release of a claim against a party in interest in exchange for consideration or extension or credit involving settlement with a party in interest
- Investment in products in which a fiduciary and/or its affiliate has an interest in the case of an automatic rollover

- Voluntary Fiduciary Correction Program class exemption (discussed in chapter 15)

Each type of exemption (statutory, individual, or class) requires satisfying the specific requirements set forth in the particular exemption. These conditions are often complex, and any plan sponsor seeking to rely on one should do so only with the advice of counsel or other professional support.

Persons who violate the prohibited-transaction rules are subject to personal liability for any losses to the plan and excise taxes of 15 percent of the amount involved. The IRS can apply a 100 percent excise tax if there is no "correction" of the transaction.[42]

POINTER: Plan fiduciaries must understand these rules and build a process to guard against prohibited transactions. To start, make a list of interested parties.

D. Civil Liability for Interference with Participant Rights

ERISA makes it unlawful for any person to discharge, fine, suspend, expel, discipline, or discriminate against anyone for exercising a right to which he or she is entitled under the plan or to interfere with the attainment of that right.[43] Participants and beneficiaries can sue for recovery of damages when a violation of this right occurs.[44] The government can assert a criminal violation if the interference is more substantial, as discussed in the next section.

E. Criminal Sanctions

The Labor Department has a criminal enforcement program that augments its civil enforcement capabilities. The mission of the criminal program is the same as the civil program, which is to protect assets of employee-benefit plans. The Labor Department seeks enforcement in the following areas:

- Prohibition against certain persons holding certain positions[45]
- Willful violations

---

[42] Code Sec. 4975. The correction of a prohibited transaction essentially involves putting the plan in the position it would have been had the transaction not occurred.

[43] ERISA Sec. 511.

[44] See Ingersoll-Rand Co. v. McClendon, 498 U.S. 133 (1990).

[45] Those convicted of certain crimes—robbery, extortion, embezzlement, perjury, certain drug offenses, labor union violations, and other ERISA offenses—may not serve as plan fiduciaries.

- Coercive interference with participant rights[46]
- Theft or embezzlement
- False statements and concealment of facts in relation to documents required by ERISA
- Offer, acceptance, or solicitation to influence the operations of an employee-benefit plan
- Mail fraud, wire fraud, and conspiracy

Labor Department sanctions for these criminal violations can be quite severe. Penalties for individuals are fines of up to $100,000 and potential imprisonment of up to ten years. Criminal penalties for entities go up to a maximum of $500,000.[47] The penalty for interference with participant rights through the willful use of actual or threatened force, violence, intimidation, restraint, coercion, or fraud ranges from $10,000 to $100,000 in fines and a maximum ten years' imprisonment.[48]

---

[46] The Labor Department will seek to impose criminal sanctions when employers interfere with employees' exercise of their rights under ERISA by willful use of actual or threatened fraud, force, or violence.

[47] ERISA Sec. 503.

[48] ERISA Sec. 511.

CHAPTER 4

Putting Together a Fiduciary Oversight Structure

Having a fiduciary oversight structure that is purposeful, comprehensive, and active should be the goal of every plan sponsor. Many plan sponsors are surprised to find that such a structure does not have to be burdensome in terms of staff resources, time, or money. In fact, for plan sponsors that would like to not do it at all, there are plan management companies that, for a reasonable fee, will take on a plan sponsor's day-to-day fiduciary responsibilities. This approach is discussed in chapter 16.

A. Considering Oversight Structure in Light of Plan Sponsor Size, Resources, and Ownership Structure

Not all governance structures are the same, nor should they be. A very large corporation may operate with the oversight and involvement of its board of directors, human resources area, finance, and separate plan committees for investments and plan administration. This is not the oversight structure you would design for a small employer, such as a sole proprietor or a small partnership; they will not very likely have any plan committees and certainly won't have a human resources area to help with the job.

The owners of small businesses are likely to be the plan administrators and trustees of their plans. If they are not trustees, the trustees are institutions that take investment directions from the owners as fiduciaries. The owners, therefore, have discretionary authority regarding all aspects of the plan. Normally, the owners make decisions regarding the plan on an informal basis and meet with the broker who sold the plan no more often than annually to go over plan investment results.

These businesses require a less formal approach to governance but one that nonetheless makes sure that they cover the five key annual obligations of fiduciary governance:

1. Plan documentation
2. Administration of the plan
3. Plan investments
4. Selection and oversight of plan service providers
5. Reporting to the government

In fact, setting up an annual agenda that covers all of these aspects of plan operations (and adhering to it) is the key for these organizations.

Larger businesses also must cover these obligations to have good governance, but their situation is both complicated and improved by the number of people who are involved in that governance. Assigning responsibilities to specific individuals, offices, or entities, together with keeping open lines of communication and information, is key. Otherwise problems and issues will not surface to the appropriate plan fiduciary.

Many times a lack of communication has cost plan sponsors dearly—situations that usually involve failures in fairly routine tasks. I have seen a sponsor's payroll department change payroll codes for the compensation data sent to the plan's TPA and used by the TPA to calculate contributions and do discrimination testing. This change resulted in the "wrong compensation" being used for these purposes, many headaches for the plan sponsor, and significant expense to straighten everything out. All this happened because of no communication between the plan sponsor's payroll and benefit-plan areas.

Pointer: The plan sponsor must understand its corporate capabilities and resources to design a fiduciary governance scheme that fits its needs. Corporate governance does not have to be, and should not be, one size fits all.

B. Allocating Responsibilities

An effort to establish effective governance does not work if the plan sponsor does not look at the plan provisions governing administration. Every plan has such provisions. Usually they will be found in a separate plan section titled, as you would expect, "Plan Administration." Sometimes they are hidden in other provisions of the plan. The plan's definitional provisions often augment and provide critical detail for the administration provisions. All of these provisions are the bedrock of effective plan governance. Plan sponsors must understand them.

A typical plan may assign the role of plan administrator to the plan sponsor unless its board of directors appoints someone else or an entity such as a committee. This is critical, because under this typical plan, the plan sponsor's board of directors is the plan administrator, responsible for administration of the plan. Because most boards do not want this responsibility, having neither the time nor the expertise for the task, the board will assign the responsibility to a committee generally made up of the sponsor's employees and officers. The role of plan administrator might also be assigned to specific individuals or positions; for example, assigning the role to the vice president of human resources is quite common. If a committee is established, the board will appoint the members of the committee.

Sometimes two committees will be appointed: one responsible for plan administration and another for plan investments. These committees may be in turn be responsible for hiring and monitoring plan service providers, including third-party administrators, accountants, consultants, attorneys, investment advisers, trustees, investment managers, custodians, and brokers. The board will have fiduciary responsibility in two aspects: (1) for the prudent appointment of committee members and (2) for the oversight of the performance of those committee members. Similarly, the committees will have responsibility for their appointments of service providers, including other fiduciaries, and those providers' performance.

Pointer: Plan sponsors must read plan documents to determine how fiduciary responsibility is originally allocated under that document. This is the only way the sponsor can begin to understand its responsibilities and set up an appropriate governance structure—or, in fact, determine whether the plan document needs to be amended to reflect the real-life allocation of responsibilities in light of the plan sponsor's business structure, culture, and capacities.

C. Setting up Committees

Assuming a plan committee (or committees) is appropriate to an employer's situation,[49] what will the committee do or have responsibility for? How will committee members be qualified for the job? How, if it at all, will committee members be protected from liability (e.g., through indemnification or fiduciary liability insurance)? Will fiduciary education be provided to newly appointed

[49] Remember, a small business such as a sole proprietorship may not want or be able to afford the formality of a formal committee. Nevertheless, that business will need to establish a governance system that will attend to all the obligations that might be allocated to a committee.

members and to current members on an ongoing basis? How big will it be? Who will be on it? How often will it meet, or will it have to meet? Who will it report to? What will it report? How will responsibilities be allocated among the committee members?

The composition of committees is important to their success. Those on investment committees obviously should be familiar with investments. That does not mean they should be as familiar as experts are with every particular aspect of plan investing. In practical terms, however, they should have enough familiarity with investing to be able to ask pertinent questions and make investment decisions based on the information provided them. Similarly, members of the plan administration committee should have an educational or business background that allows them to comprehend the various plan administration issues that may come before the committee.[50] Often these committees will have a VP of human resources as a member, as well as someone from payroll or finance to provide plans administration expertise.[51]

Pointer: When a plan sponsor establishes separate investment and plan administration committees, it is desirable to appoint some individuals as members of both committees. This cross-fertilization may prevent lapses in oversight and enhance recognition of issues that might not otherwise be discovered or discussed.

Pointer: A plan invested in employer stock that is publicly traded should avoid having on the committees plan sponsor executives who are "insiders" under the securities laws, since these individuals would be conflicted between their obligation to act in the exclusive interests of the plan and the legal prohibition under the securities laws not to make public material, nonpublic information. This is often a hard pill to swallow for high-level executives who traditionally have been significant presences on these committees.

Committee responsibilities are not likely to be spelled out in sufficient detail (and sometimes not at all) in the plan document to be of much use in the actual oversight and administration of a plan. This is where a written committee charter is indispensable. It supplements the plan document, answers many of the questions raised in the first paragraph, and makes practical the responsibilities that often seem fairly abstract in the plan document.

---

[50] In any matter where a committee does not have requisite expertise, the committee must consult with the appropriate subject matter expert.

[51] Because employee-benefit plans, in particular 401(k) plans, are so complex, newly appointed committee members should be provided with a fiduciary education that includes a review of the plan itself, the various laws applicable to the plan, and the obligations of committee members as fiduciaries under ERISA.

Pointer: There is a fine line between enough and too much detail in committee charters and procedures. There should be sufficient detail to guide plan oversight and administration, but not so much that plan fiduciaries trip over minute details. A good plan-governance expert can help employers establish properly balanced documentation—and perhaps avoid fiduciary breach litigation.

D. Reporting and Communication: Key to Accountability

Any good committee structure must require timely and complete reports from the service providers for which the committee has oversight responsibilities. An investment committee needs investment-performance reports from those responsible for investments, including trustees, investment managers, and advisers. A plan administration committee similarly needs reports from TPAs, consultants, CPAs, attorneys, and its own human resources area. It is up to the committee to establish with the service provider the frequency and form of communication.

Equally important is the committee's reporting up to the entity that established the committee or appointed its members. Typically, a committee reports to the board of directors and should do so at least annually. Such reporting has benefits because it enables the board (or the appointing fiduciary) to fulfill both its oversight and its monitoring obligation to the plan. Remember, the appointing fiduciary has responsibility for the initial appointment and for monitoring the performance of the appointee. Periodic reporting supports accountability, surfacing of problems, and more effective plan management.

Pointer: Each plan structure is different, which means a committee may need to report to its board more frequently than annually. For example, where the committee has general oversight responsibility of an investment manager but the board retains authority to appoint the manager, the committee may find it needs to report to the board more frequently. Or if the committee finds the manager's performance shoddy or there has been a significant change in manager personnel, reports must be prepared and actions may need to be taken immediately to replace the manager.

E. Establishing an Annual Agenda

As mentioned previously, fiduciary oversight involves five annual obligations. (See section A above.) Each area or item must be on the annual agenda of the plan sponsor, committee(s), or other responsible fiduciary. Normally this responsibility is with a plan committee or with committees responsible for the particular subject matter area. For example, some plan sponsors have one committee responsible for plan administration and investments. Others will allocate those responsibilities to two separate committees. Smaller plan sponsors may not have a committee at all and the responsibility may reside in the owner or with the CFO.

The time of year for these items to be placed on the calendar will reflect the size and complexity of the organization and the timing requirements for the specific area of plan responsibility. For example, amendments to a plan required by law or government regulation must be made by the end of the year in which the amendment is effective. Thus, it is a good idea to focus on this item in the first half of the year to allow ample time to get the amendment to the board for approval. Early board approval also is necessary to prepare appropriate employee communications and adjust summary plan descriptions.

Annual returns must be filed by July 31, if not on extension,[52] for calendar year plans. TPAs normally prepare the return for the signature of the plan administrator. This item, then, should normally be put in the first or second calendar quarter. The committee wants assurance that the preparation process has begun, that the TPA has all necessary information to complete the return and that the work is progressing. If an independent qualified plan auditor's (IQPA) report must be filed with the return, the committee needs to know that the accountant's work has begun and that it is progressing satisfactorily.

Plan administration items such as problems with distributions, discrimination testing, plan loans, and the deposit of salary-deferral contributions might well be on the calendar on a quarterly basis. Consideration of fiduciary services and fees can be once-a-year events, as can plan effectiveness reviews and participant education plans.

Pointer: Once a calendar is established, there is no going back. In other words, a committee's actions (or non-action) will be judged, in part, against the calendar. Failure to follow a calendar will be viewed as a fiduciary failure by regulators and plaintiff's attorneys. Disciplined behavior and adherence to the calendar and to other prudent governance processes pays big dividends in terms of defending against regulator actions and employee claims.

F. Holding Effective Meetings

It's important, as with any business meeting, that plan committee meetings be run efficiently and effectively in the interests of the plan and to protect the interests of plan participants and beneficiaries. No one wants to waste time, and no one has to waste time -- with proper organization. My experience in advising plan sponsors tells me this can be achieved under the following circumstances:

[52] See chapter 14 for more information on filing dates and extensions of time to file.

- Meetings should be regularly scheduled and of sufficient length to adequately and completely analyze the matters under consideration.
- Notice of the meeting and adequate information concerning all important matters requiring attention, together with a detailed agenda and copies of minutes of the previous meeting and of any committee or co-fiduciary meetings, should be distributed sufficiently in advance for meaningful review.
- Fiduciaries should carefully and critically analyze meeting materials *before* meetings.
- Meetings should be conducted in an atmosphere that encourages frank and full discussion. Ample opportunity to actively question and challenge advisers and one another should be provided.
- The chairperson should run the meeting to both move things along and make sure that all agenda items are adequately discussed.
- The committee must control the agenda and the discussion. The broker or investment advisor must not run the meetings.
- Minutes should be maintained and should document clearly and concisely the matters discussed; record any recommendations given by advisors; and set forth resolutions approved, actions taken, and decisions made. Minutes should be reviewed before finalization by the fiduciaries and legal counsel. Fiduciaries should carefully review not only the minutes of meetings they attend, but also the minutes of any meetings they did not attend.

POINTER: Prepare meeting minutes to generally state that a particular discussion took place and the result of the discussion. There is no requirement that the minutiae of the discussion be recorded, and, in fact, such a discussion could be quite detrimental in litigation. Keep it brief.

G. Isolating Plan Sponsor Issues from Fiduciary Issues

Issues relating to plan administration are not generally subject to attorney-client privilege. This means that in any potential litigation, committee deliberations concerning these matters would be available to the plaintiff (e.g., a participant) in the litigation.

Discussions that relate solely to settlor or plan sponsor responsibilities may be privileged. These include discussions concerning changes in the plan's design or its termination.

POINTER: Leave discussions of settlor interests off committee agendas. Some employers find it useful to a have a benefits attorney present at committee meetings to ward off discussions that become settlor in nature and to provide advice on other issues before the committee. Because attorney-client privilege is not easy to determine, it is always recommended to consult with an ERISA or employee-benefits attorney when in doubt.

H. Using Compliance Audits

An independent and unbiased third-party evaluation, or "audit," can be a valuable tool in identifying problems and weaknesses in a plan's oversight and administration. Such a review could include an assessment of all or some of the following:

- Document compliance
- Communication to participants
- Plan administration standards
- Service provider performance
- Investment management and performance
- Safeguards against self-dealing and party-in-interest transactions

Each of these areas is discussed in more detail later in this book.

I. Reviewing Plan Effectiveness

Annually, the plan sponsor should engage in a review of the plan's effectiveness in achieving plan sponsor goals, participant income-replacement goals, participant education, and investment-advice programs.

CHAPTER 5

Managing Internal Fiduciaries

Plan sponsor officers and employees may become what I call "internal fiduciaries" to their plans.[53] This status arises because (1) the plan document assigns it to someone (for example, to a committee or plan sponsor officer), (2) someone falls into it because of how they act in relation to the plan (see chapter 1), or (3) they are appointed. This chapter focuses largely on appointments and the oversight of those appointed.

A. General Considerations in Appointing Fiduciaries

Appointing fiduciaries—usually boards or their committees—have an important role to fill in plan management. After all, the appointees' decisions will affect how well plan participants are prepared for retirement. Appointments must therefore be carefully considered.

There are three key aspects in the appointment of internal fiduciaries to plan committees. They are the:

1. quality of the candidates appointed,
2. training provided to these employees, and
3. protections they are provided for the risks they assume with the appointment.

[53] This not a technical or legal term but my own way of distinguishing those fiduciaries within the plan sponsor. By way of contrast, a trust company or bank acting as plan trustee would be considered an "outside" fiduciary.

On the opposite side of the coin, executive and employee candidates should have the following concerns as they consider accepting an appointment:

1. whether they are qualified for the job and can commit to it,
2. whether the plan sponsor will provide fiduciary training, and
3. how will the plan sponsor protect them from liability.

An additional concern for potential appointees is the "what am I getting into?" question. They should want to know the general condition of the plan and any known problems before accepting the appointment. Nobody wants to step into a room full of snakes without at least being warned.

B. Qualifying Committee Members

I have found in advising plan sponsor boards that the following elements are critical to establishing an individual's qualification for appointment as a fiduciary:

- Federal law prohibits individuals from holding the position of a plan fiduciary if they have been convicted of various criminal offenses.[54] Therefore, the board or the entity qualifying a candidate should ask the candidate to affirm that he or she has not committed any criminal acts that preclude him or her from being a plan fiduciary.

POINTER: For maximum protection, some plan sponsors will authorize criminal background checks of fiduciary or committee candidates.

- Fiduciaries must be able and willing to exercise independent judgment. They should not be selected based on corporate position, personal relationships, or other potentially irrelevant factors. People who are likely to acquiesce to the plan sponsor should not be appointed.
- The candidate's other commitments should be examined to ensure that the person has adequate time to serve as a fiduciary for the plan. For example, if the responsibilities of the individual's regular job cannot possibly allow the individual to adequately exercise the role of plan fiduciary, that person should not be appointed. Conversely, if the individual determines that the plan sponsor would not provide him or her with the time and resources necessary to fulfill the responsibility, the individual ought to refuse the appointment.

[54] ERISA Sec. 411.

- Any conflict of interest that could affect an individual's ability to act for the exclusive benefit of plan participants and beneficiaries must be considered in qualifying a candidate. For example, an executive for the plan sponsor whose brother is a service provider to the plan is not a good candidate. If a conflict exists, the individual should not be appointed unless a way is found to eliminate the conflict.
- Larger plan sponsors may wish to use their plan administration committees to vet candidates on behalf of the board. This vetting results in a recommendation of candidates to the board. The board can rely on the expertise of the committee and avoid spending its energies in an area where it is not likely to have much expertise.

C. Formalizing Appointments, Resignations, and Removals of Committee Members

The need to document fiduciary activities is a theme repeated throughout this book. Failure to document can lead to troublesome results. Sometimes a board will formally appoint an individual without receiving a corresponding written acceptance of the appointment. Other times, committee members just disappear. This happens frequently when a committee member retires or leaves to take a job with another employer. In these situations there is fiduciary risk; plan matters may go unattended, leaving the departing executive and the plan sponsor with exposure to potential liabilities.

To avoid these problems, the appointment, resignation, and removal of committee members and other fiduciaries should always be documented as follows:

- Board appointments should be memorialized in written resolutions of the board, followed by a letter to the appointee notifying him or her of the appointment and requesting written acknowledgement of the acceptance of the appointment.
- Board removals should be memorialized in written resolutions of the board, followed by a letter notifying the individual of the removal and requesting written acknowledgement of the removal.
- Resignations should be submitted in writing to the board or to the appropriate officer of the plan sponsor and should not be effective earlier than is reasonable for the proper protection of the interests of the plan.

D. Indemnification and Insurance: Maximizing Officer and Employee Legal Protection

Executives and employees who become plan committee members or fiduciaries take on significant exposure to liability. They may make mistakes, act negligently, or not act when they should have. Even if there is no failure on the part of the fiduciary, a participant or the Labor Department may still sue the fiduciary. The costs of defending against a lawsuit can be substantial. Following are important considerations related to indemnification and insurance for fiduciaries.

Plan sponsor and executive concerns. It is appropriate and necessary for internal fiduciaries to consider how they will be protected before agreeing to take the job. Likewise must consider how they are protecting their executives from personal liability. A sponsor may determine to protect employees by promising to indemnify them. Indemnification is essentially a guarantee against any loss that the employee might suffer from the exercise of his or her responsibilities as a fiduciary.

Legal approaches to indemnification. A plan sponsor may "promise" indemnification in one of these ways:

- In an amendment to its articles of incorporation
- In an amendment to its bylaws
- In a separate agreement with the executive
- In the plan document

Extent of indemnification. The extent and manner of the indemnification can vary. Common indemnification provisions might include advancement of defense expenses, shifting the burden of proof to the sponsoring organization to prove that the fiduciary is not entitled to indemnification, or requiring the sponsoring organization to reimburse the fiduciary for any expenses incurred in defending a claim against the plan or sponsoring organization.

Funding the indemnification. A promise to indemnify is not worth anything if no assets back up the promise. This is often the case because it seems when plans are in trouble and fiduciaries are sued the plan sponsor has an underlying financial problem. Therefore, many sponsors seek to "secure" the promise to indemnify, using any of the following techniques:

- Establishing a reserve fund
- Purchasing a surety bond, a letter of credit, or other similar financial instrument
- Purchasing ERISA fiduciary liability insurance

Pointer: The indemnification provided should be worked out with the advice of knowledgeable corporate and benefits counsel and, if insurance is used to fund the promise, also with the advice of a knowledgeable insurance consultant.

ERISA Fiduciary liability insurance. Plan sponsors often purchase fiduciary liability insurance to fund the indemnification. The risk is then transferred to the insurance company, and there is no worry about the plan sponsor becoming insolvent or not having sufficient available cash flow to pay losses and expenses the fiduciary may incur. Insurance can also offer executives protection against changes in applicable law or unilateral changes by the sponsor to plan documents or corporate bylaws. If the insurance company is the payment source, executives will be protected against outright refusals to pay that have no basis in any documentation.

Who purchases the ERISA fiduciary liability policy? Polices may also be purchased by the plan on behalf of the fiduciary. A problem with this approach, for employees and officers, is that the plan is required to recoup its losses from the fiduciary if a breach of fiduciary duty occurs. For this reason, the plan sponsor, rather than the plan, is the entity that generally purchases this coverage.

What about D&O or Directors & Officers policies? ERISA fiduciary liability coverage is not normally provided in a directors and officers' policy. Plan sponsors are often confused about this, believing the D&O policy provides the coverage. The coverage can be provided in a rider to the regular D&O policy.

Pointer: Employers should periodically review with their insurance advisors or agents their ERISA fiduciary liability coverage to determine that the coverage does what they intend it to do.

ERISA fidelity bonds: no ERISA fiduciary liability protection. Federal law requires covered plans to purchase a bond on any fiduciary and all other persons who handle the plan's monies.[55] The bonding requirement should not be confused with ERISA fiduciary liability insurance. Fidelity bonds reimburse the *plan* and only for losses arising from dishonesty; they do not protect fiduciaries against claims made against them. A bond does not protect a plan fiduciary from fiduciary liability.

E. Fiduciary Training

No responsible parent sends a teenager out in the family car for the first time without a lesson. Yet it is common for newly appointed fiduciaries to be sent out to drive the heavy machinery of a 401(k) or 403(b) plan without even an admonishment to drive slowly or obey all stop signs. Both plan sponsors and their appointed fiduciaries have a strong interest in "not driving off the road" and in understanding the fiduciary

[55] This requirement is under ERISA Sec. 412.

role and being qualified for the job—the sponsor because it has liability for the appointment, and fiduciaries because they are directly liable for their failures.

Fiduciary training or education must have two basic components. It must communicate the following:

- **The law**—the basic statutory and regulatory rules governing 401(k) and 403(b) plans. These rules include tax qualification and taxation of distributions under the Internal Revenue Code and the general rules of fiduciary responsibility that apply to the plan and its fiduciaries. (The major areas of fiduciary responsibility are discussed in chapter 2, "What Is the Nature of Fiduciary Responsibility?")

POINTER: ERISA allows officers or employees of plan sponsors to act simultaneously in two conflicting capacities. That is, as officers and employees they have a duty of loyalty to their employer and as a plan fiduciary they have a duty to act in the exclusive interests of the plan. These loyalties may come into direct conflict. Thus fiduciaries must avoid situations where these interests are in direct conflict.[56] Fiduciary training should teach the appointee how to recognize, avoid, and find solutions in these situations. Avoidance approaches might include not participating in plan decisions in which they or the plan sponsor have an interest (recusal) or by other means, such as appointing an independent fiduciary.

- **The plan**—Copies of plan documents should be provided to the fiduciary so that he or she can familiarize him or herself with the plan's eligibility, contribution, vesting, distribution, and administrative provisions. The fiduciary should be provided with a list of key players including trustees, custodians, TPAs, investment advisers, accountants, attorneys, and other consultants to the plan and a description of what they do. Internal personnel or departments responsible for administering the plan or having some connection to the plan, such as a payroll department should also be identified.

POINTER: Fiduciary training or education should come, at least in part, before the appointment. In other words, the candidate, like any other individual applying for a job, ought to try to understand, before the appointment, what the job and its challenges are. Similarly, the plan sponsor wants to know whether a candidate has determined that he or she can do the job and is willing to accept its challenges.

---

[56] ERISA section 403; Amato v. Western Union Int'l, Inc., 773 Fed 1402 (2d Cir. 1985) cert. denied, 459 U.S. 1113 (1986).

Fiduciary education doesn't end with the first driver's lesson. Periodically, perhaps annually, appointees should be updated on any developments in the laws or regulations having a bearing on their responsibilities under the plan.

Pointer: Many consulting companies provide initial and updated training for internal fiduciaries at very reasonable cost. Webinar trainings are also available at even less cost through organizations such as the Society for Human Resources Management (SHRM), Profit Sharing Council of America (PSCA), and others. The US Department of Labor also holds meetings across the country for plan sponsors interested in learning about their plan responsibilities. Some plan sponsors manage to incorporate a bit of fiduciary training at every committee meeting.

F. Compensation for Fiduciaries Receiving Full-Time Pay from Plan Sponsor

Care should be exercised to avoid paying compensation from the plan's assets to fiduciaries that are full-time employees of the plan sponsor—a practice prohibited under federal law.[57] This does not preclude payment from plan assets of the properly incurred expenses of these individuals. For example, expenses incurred for fiduciary training could be a properly incurred expense provided the cost is reasonable.

G. Human Resources Staff

Human resource personnel often are actively involved with plan administration, even when a third-party administrator is primarily responsible for plan administration. Human resource staff solves problems and works with TPAs and others on a variety of tasks, such as transmittal of census information (such as dates of hire, hours of service, compensation), participant salary-deferral election information, and the like. In these tasks they will be resolving various plan issues. For the most part staff will be acting as non-fiduciaries. If any staff is appointed in a fiduciary capacity, the plan sponsor and the appointee should have the same concerns as they would have in the appointment of an executive to a committee. See the discussion at Section A above.

In whatever capacity human resources staff acts, appropriate and periodic reporting to a plan committee or other overseeing fiduciary is requisite.

[57] Labor Regulation Sec. 2550.408(c)-2(b)(2).

CHAPTER 6

Hiring Plan Service Providers

Plan sponsors entrust plan service providers with large amounts of money and put their employees' retirement futures into their hands. It is only right (and the expectation of the law) that plan sponsors exercise great care when they hire service providers. This chapter describes the process that goes into a "good" hire.

A. Managing Fees and Costs

When hiring a service provider, there is perhaps no more important task for internal plan fiduciaries than the management of plan costs and expenses. Plan fiduciaries are under a general affirmative duty to act in the best interests of plan participants and beneficiaries.[58] They are also subject to specific obligations to engage service providers only if those providers are providing services necessary to the plan's administration and at no more than reasonable cost.[59]

Cost becomes even more critical when it is understood that in most plans today, costs are paid from plan assets and not by the plan sponsor. It is estimated that a 1 percent difference in fees and expenses will reduce investment return over a thirty-five-year period by 28 percent.[60] Thus, costs and fees have a bottom-line

[58] ERISA Sec. 404(a).

[59] ERISA Sec. 408(b)(2; Labor Department Regulation Section 2550.408c-2.

[60] See "A Look at 401(k) Plan Fees," US Department of Labor, at http://www.dol.gov/ebsa/publications/401k_employee.html, as visited on February 15, 2014.

impact on participant account balances at retirement. Of course, fees (the "reasonableness" thereof) are very much influenced by the quality and extent of the services provided, which we'll discuss in detail later in this chapter. First, let's talk about how plans pay service providers.

B. Plan Fee Categories

Fees may be categorized as one of three types: (1) administrative service fees, (2) investment fees, and (3) individual service fees.

Administrative service fees include those for third-party administration; record keeping; trustee, custodial, and legal services; and accounting. The modern 401(k) or 403(b) plan may also offer other services, including educational seminars, investment advice, retirement planning software, electronic access to information, telephonic voice response systems, daily valuation, and online transactions. These fees may be paid by the plan or plan sponsor or through investment fees deducted from investment return.

POINTER: Administrative services are not free. **They are paid directly from plan assets, deducted from investment return or paid by the plan sponsor.** Using investment returns to pay administrative fees is sometimes not recognized or understood by plan sponsors, leaving them to think that administrative services are provided for free. Nothing could be further from the truth.

Investment fees are applied as a percentage of assets invested and are taken indirectly from plan investment returns. These fees will generally be a plan's greatest expense and fall into three general categories:

- Sales charges that are transaction costs for buying and selling shares
- Investment-advice or management fees for managing the assets in the investment fun
- Other fees for record keeping, furnishing statements, toll-free numbers, and the like

Individual transaction service fees are fees charged directly to an individual participant's account for such things as taking a loan or a hardship distribution, processing a domestic relations order, or for brokerage windows.

C. Common Investments and Related Fees

Common investments are mutual funds and common or collective trusts. They are considered to offer significant value because they pool the investments of large numbers of individual investors. Such a pooling arrangement makes it possible to diversify investments, achieve economies of scale, and lower costs related to their professional management and investment. Financial institutions that offer these pooled arrangements include mutual funds, banks, insurance companies, and hedge funds.

Mutual funds are owned by their investor shareholders and are managed by an investment adviser under an investment policy. Detailed in the fund's prospectus, the investment policy sets forth the fund's investment objectives. The fund's adviser receives a management fee for services to the fund, which is paid from the fund's assets. Additional fees may be charged as an expense of the fund. These include:

- *Sales charges.* Sales charges are fees charged to the plan investor when shares are purchased or when they are sold. Charges for buying apply when there is an investment in Class A shares (front-end load), and charges for selling when there is a sale of Class B shares (back-end load). A front-end-load fund imposes a fee on the initial purchase of the share (e.g., 3 percent) and an ongoing 12b-1 fee (see the discussion of 12b-1 fees below). Back-end-load funds charge a fee if shares are sold before a certain period elapses. These share classes are not typically offered in 401(k) or 403(b) plans. Occasionally one may see C shares as plan investments. These shares have both front-end load and back-end load characteristics.
- *Built-in fees.* The most common share classes sold to 401(k) and 403(b) plans are Class I and Class R shares. These share classes do not impose any sales charges. Class I shares are offered to institutional investors—such as 401(k) and 403(b) plans—with minimum investments of $1 million or more and are typically lower cost. Class R shares are designed specifically for retirement plans, and they may or may not be as low cost as I shares because mutual-fund families may build additional charges into these shares for costs such as retirement-plan management, record keeping, and administrative expenses. Sometimes these shares come in subclasses, such as R-1, R-2, and so on, with substantially different fees.

POINTER: Responsible plan fiduciaries must make it their business to know share classes and the true costs associated with them. The plan sponsor must ask the following questions: What share class is being recommended? What are the expenses associated with it? If a cheaper share class is available, why isn't that class being used? A broker's recommendation to purchase Class A or B shares should be viewed with great skepticism and evaluated thoroughly.

Pointer: A particular share class may initially be perfectly appropriate and reasonably priced, and then due to increases in plan assets become unreasonable. Plan sponsors and advisors must make themselves aware of the break points. These are the points at which fees reduce based on asset size. For example, asset based fees might be 40 basis points up to two million dollars in assets and 30 basis point for plans with assets in excess of two million dollars when placed in a different asset class. It therefore pays to know when a breakpoint has been reached. The vendor won't always tell you.

- *12b-1 fees.* These are fees paid out of fund assets for brokers' commissions, advertising, and other costs of promoting the fund to investors. Often these fees will be used (directed) for the payment of plan administrative expenses or returned to participant accounts as an "investment" of the plan. Importantly, the plan sponsor must find out and understand where these fees are going. This information will tell the plan sponsor a great deal about true plan costs.
- *Subtransfer agent fees.* Known as "sub-TA fees" or "shareholder servicing fees," these are fees paid by trust companies, banks, and mutual-fund companies to other entities to track buy-and-sell orders and to credit them to the appropriate participant accounts.
- *Soft dollars.* Technically soft dollars or "excess commissions" consist of revenue paid to brokerages under Securities Exchange Commission (SEC) Rule 28(e). For example, a mutual fund may offer to pay for research from a brokerage firm by executing trades at the brokerage. In other words, soft dollars add to the broker's total compensation.
- *Target-date mutual fund fees.* Target-date mutual funds assume a specific retirement date, say 2025, and often may be composed of investments in other mutual funds. These funds may have two sets of fees: one fee for managing the funds within the fund and another set of fees for managing the separate funds within the target-date fund. An important question for the plan sponsor to ask: is the plan sponsor overpaying for the investment given the two sets of fees and as compared to a single mutual fund investment that does the same thing?

Pointer: The plan sponsor must check to see whether it has received a disclosure of each type of fee. The sponsor should ask its providers if they receive soft-dollar benefits from the mutual funds and what soft-dollar benefits they have received or continue to receive. Each of these fees is required to be disclosed in writing by service providers. These disclosure requirements are discussed later in this chapter.

Collective investment funds are trust funds managed by a bank or trust company that pools the investments of plans and similar investors, such as individual retirement accounts. Each plan investor has a proportionate interest in the assets of the fund. Investment management and administrative fees charged are incurred by these funds, but there are no sales charges at either the time of purchase or when the investment in the fund is sold.

Insurance Company Products. Through variable annuity contracts, insurance companies can offer investment alternatives that are similar to or mirror identically specific mutual funds, giving participants a full range of investment alternatives. Because variable annuities are an insurance product, they may include insurance features not present in other investment products. Insurance-related charges associated with the investment alternatives include sales charges, mortality risk charges, and costs related to issuing and administering the contract. More recently insurance companies have begun offering investment lineups that consist of shares of the mutual funds themselves. In other words, there are a wide variety of arrangements available to plan sponsors through these companies. And fees under these arrangements may or may not be higher than for other types of arrangements.

Pointer: Plan sponsors using or considering variable annuity or other types of insurance company products must consider what they are being sold and whether the higher cost, if any, is justified. Generally, for larger plans with significant assets, an annuity-based product cannot be justified. For smaller employers, use of the product may be a sound choice. The only way to find out for sure is to comparison-shop against non-annuity offerings.

Hedge-fund investments. This type of investment is not common in 401(k) plans (and not available to 403(b) plans except through mutual fund investments), but may be coming into vogue. Also called "private equity funds," these funds use different investment strategies. Some seek performance that meets or exceed market indices with lower volatility and others look to exploit market indices. Some do no hedging at all. Fees under these arrangements involve a management and a performance fee. A common arrangement is an assets management fee of 2 percent and a performance fee based on 20 percent of the gains over a minimal specified base return—sometimes called the "hurdle rate."

Exchange traded funds. This type of investment, also called an ETF, is a security that tracks an index, commodity, or index fund. It trades like a stock with changes in value throughout the investment day as shares are bought and sold. These funds are not commonly held in 401(k) plans and may not be held at all by 403(b) plans.

D. Bundled Provider Arrangements

Some mutual fund or insurance company providers offer a total package of services in one-stop shopping arrangements. These arrangements are very common in the industry. The services include investments, record keeping, administration, and participant education. Administrative services usually include annual return (Form 5500) preparation, preparation of plan documents and amendments, and trustee or custodial services. Some providers ally with investment management entities to increase the range of participant investment choices. Fees for the services may be paid out of plan assets, from 12b-1 and other fees, or by the plan sponsor.

POINTER: Bundled arrangements can be tricky and may be more expensive than readily apparent. This is because providers tend to load investment recommendations with their own "proprietary" funds to increase their own revenue, often at the cost of better-performing, nonproprietary investment alternatives.

POINTER: Plan sponsors and their advisers must carefully evaluate the level of services provided. For example, there are payroll companies that offer bundled services that assume no responsibility for the quality of the data used to administer the plan or for important plan design determinations that may impact the tax qualification of 401(k) plans and costs to the plan sponsor. In other words, their service levels are very low.

E. Unbundled Provider Arrangements

These provider arrangements, sometimes called "open source architecture," represent the à la carte approach to plan services and vendors. In these arrangements, plan sponsors separately pick the third-party administrator, custodian, recordkeeper, education provider, and other service providers. Each vendor bills separately for the service provided to the plan. Fees for the services may be paid out of plan assets, from 12b-1 and other fees, or by the plan sponsor. The format allows plans to select investments from hundreds of mutual fund and ETFs without impacting a provider's fees to the plan.

F. Due Diligence on the Service Provider

Plan fiduciaries have a responsibility for determining the quality of the services the provider can be expected to provide. On any responsible plan fiduciary's checklist should be the following:

- Whether the vendor has experience with plans of this one's size, type, and complexity
- Whether the vendor has the staff and infrastructure to meet its servicing commitments, including information about the identity, experience, and qualifications of the staff members who will be handling the plan
- Any recent litigation or enforcement action that has been taken against the vendor, and whether the vendor has fiduciary liability or other insurance protective of the plan
- A description of the vendor's business practices, including whether it has any procedures or processes for the services it provides
- Information about the vendor's financial condition
- Whether there are any outstanding claims or lawsuits against the vendor

G. Service Provider Agreements

Service provider agreements are a very important but an often-ignored part of the provider selection process for both 401(k) and 403(b) plans. I have seen two typical situations: there is no written agreement governing the terms of the service arrangement, or there is one but the employer has not read it. The plan sponsor must have a written agreement, and it should be negotiated with care. There is no excuse for not having a negotiated, written agreement. In fact, if your arrangement is with a covered service provider there *must* be an agreement. See the discussion at chapter 7. There is never ever any excuse for not reading a service provider agreement.

Agreements should cover explicitly five major areas:

1. **Description of services provided.** This should (i) describe which administrative functions remain with the plan sponsor and which are assigned to the service provider, (ii) explicitly set out each service the service provider will be providing, and (iii) identify any deadlines for performance of services and provide for consequences if a deadline is missed. If the service provider is a fiduciary, this should be stated in the agreement.

POINTER: Confusion over who is responsible for what can be especially expensive for plan sponsors—for example, if they rely on the provider for an important task the provider is not in fact doing. The plan sponsor needs to know exactly what the sponsor's responsibilities are and what the service provider's are.

2. **Compensation and fee disclosures.** How service provider compensation is determined and when it is paid should be set out in the agreement. Moreover, since the law requires service providers to disclose fee and service information to the plan sponsor, this obligation should be set out in the agreement. This will give the plan sponsor a contractual basis for challenging a service provider's failure to comply with the rules.

POINTER: Plan sponsors became subject to a new rule[61] in 2012 that requires them to make explicit disclosures to participants of plan-wide fees that affect the value of their accounts and of fees that are specific to individual participant accounts (such as fees charged for participant loans and the like). It is wise to include in the agreement what the provider obligates itself to with respect to these disclosures. For example, will the provider prepare and deliver them? This is something the plan sponsor very much needs to know.

3. **Limitation of liability and indemnification.** These provisions of a service agreement should make clear that the plan and plan sponsor are protected from the service provider's wrongful acts and breach of fiduciary duty. Many standard service provider contracts will limit the service provider's liability quite substantially. The Labor Department permits plan fiduciaries to agree to limitation of liability provisions.[62] But there is a limit to what a plan fiduciary should agree to. For example, I have seen service provider liability limited to an amount equal to the last quarter's fees. Such a limited indemnification generally would not be sufficient to cover the plan's costs or losses. This is not reasonable.

POINTER: Don't do business with anyone who won't stand by his or her work without limitation.

4. **ERISA bond, errors and omissions coverage, and fiduciary liability coverage.** The service provider agreement should contain representations that the provider has purchased an ERISA bond, has errors and omissions coverage. When the service provider is a fiduciary, the fiduciary should have and represent that it has fiduciary liability coverage.

---

[61] Labor Department Reg. Sec. 2550.404a-5. These requirements are discussed in chapter 13.

[62] Labor Department Advisory Opinion 2002-08A.

5. **Termination of the service agreement.** This part of the agreement is particularly important because on termination of the agreement, the plan sponsor will need full cooperation in smoothly transitioning to the next provider. These provisions permit the plan sponsor to terminate the arrangement on reasonably short notice and without penalty.

POINTER: Because covered service providers or CSPs are required to make certain fee and service description disclosures prior to the execution of an agreement, the plan sponsor should make sure it obtains the disclosures during the negotiation period and well before an agreement is executed. See chapter 7 for more detail.

There are many other issues that ought to be considered in connection with a service provider agreement. These include: (1) choice of the state law that will apply in the case of a dispute and where a suit can be brought, (2) electronic communications, (3) and protection of personal information under state privacy laws.

This discussion is not meant to be exhaustive, but rather to give an outline of things plan sponsors should consider when entering into a service agreement. There is no substitute for retaining a qualified benefits attorney to review or to assist with the negotiation of the agreement.

H. Detecting Conflicts of Interest and Avoiding Prohibited Transactions

Service provider arrangements can pose challenges to plan sponsors because they often involve multiple related service providers. One example is a mutual-fund bundled arrangement or platform that typically involves a broker getting paid by the mutual-fund company, the mutual-fund company itself, an affiliated third-party administrator, and an affiliated trust company—all sharing revenue with each other. These arrangements make self-dealing (i.e., taking excessive compensation) hard to detect.

Plan sponsors have a better chance under the comprehensive disclosure rules described in chapter 7, "Determining the Reasonableness of Fees," but still have to work hard to determine how money and fees are flowing among those affiliated companies. As mentioned in chapter 7, employers can start by preparing a list of the parties involved in the arrangement, determining what those parties do and how they might use their authority to benefit themselves and/or an affiliated entity to the detriment of the plan.

I. Legal Counsel Review

It is a good practice to retain legal counsel for the review of service provider agreements. This review can often result in a clearer expression of the respective rights and obligations of the parties and the other benefits as described in section G above. Hiring an attorney is money well spent.

J. Documented Process

The process of retaining a service provider or obtaining services should be documented. In cases where the value of services or products sought is significant, plan fiduciaries may wish to obtain multiple proposals using an RFP (request for proposal) process. In any event, information from the vendor should be sought, carefully reviewed, and retained in the records of the plan. A record of fiduciary deliberations regarding the decision to use a particular service provider also should be retained.

K. Subsequent Periodic Review of Providers and Agreements

Fiduciaries must periodically review the performance of service providers and the reasonableness of fees. Is the service provider performing as described under the agreement? Are any services provided no longer needed? Are they still being provided at reasonable cost to the plan?

The plan sponsor or plan administrative committee should make this periodic review part of its operating procedures, document the review, and take any actions reasonably required as a result of the review.

CHAPTER 7

Determining the Reasonableness of Fees

Since the enactment of ERISA in 1974, responsible plan fiduciaries have been under a legal obligation to determine the reasonableness of compensation and fees for services provided to a plan. This chapter describes what this means to plan sponsors in terms of service provider's obligations to provide the sponsor with fee and service information.

A. Informational Requirements and Standards of Care

Implicit in the ERISA required responsibility to determine fee reasonableness is the fiduciary's obligation to seek all information relevant to that determination. But the law provided no guidance on how to do this. Plan sponsors were left on their own to determine what information they needed to understand very complex 401(k) and 403(b) plan fee arrangements. This changed in 2012 when rules became effective[63] requiring for the first time certain covered service providers to provide specified fee and description of services information to responsible plan fiduciaries.[64] Under the rules, no such service provider arrangement can be considered reasonable unless the required disclosures are made.

[63] Labor Department Reg. Sec. 408c-2.

[64] The sanction on the service provider for failing to provide this information is the imposition of excise taxes under Code Section 4975 the removal of the service provider and the return to the plan of perhaps all or a portion of the fees paid.

This regulation also requires responsible plan fiduciaries to make a determination of the information's adequacy under the new requirements. If the information provided is not sufficient, the responsible plan fiduciary must ask the provider to furnish it.[65]

Pointer: Plan sponsor fiduciaries must determine that the providers' information is complete under the rules. To prevent this responsibility from falling through the cracks, a committee member, officer, or some other appropriately responsible person should be assigned the task as the "responsible fiduciary."

The informational requirement does not necessarily satisfy the fiduciary's obligation to make a determination on the reasonableness of fees. Even if the information provided under the regulation otherwise satisfies the new disclosure rules, the fiduciary remains obligated to request additional information or clarification from the service provider to understand their fees and services.

Pointer: Plan sponsor fiduciaries *must* keep in mind that the information provided by their service providers is the minimum required under Labor Department rules. The plan fiduciary may need more information to meet its fiduciary obligations.

It is important to understand the basis of the new rules and the implications of failing to comply. The disclosure requirement falls under the prohibited transactions provisions of ERISA. Under those provisions, as strange as it may seem, a service provider engages in a prohibited transaction when it provides service to a plan.[66] This obviously unworkable situation (Plans need service providers!) is saved by a statutory exemption that allows it, as long as the arrangement is reasonable and necessary and the provider receives no more than reasonable compensation.[67]

That exemption says that if the required or mandatory disclosures are made and the arrangement is otherwise reasonable, the provision of the service is not prohibited and a breach of fiduciary duty does not result. On the other hand, if there is a mandatory disclosure failure and the plan sponsor fails to do anything about it, the plan sponsor (responsible plan fiduciary) will have engaged in a prohibited transaction and breach his or her duty. In other words, until the plan sponsor is fully informed of its service providers' fees and has documented how it found them reasonable, the plan sponsor has not done its job.

---

[65] Further failure to provide the information requires the responsible plan fiduciary to report the failure to the Labor Department.

[66] ERISA Sec. 406(a).

[67] ERISA Sec. 408(b)(2).

B. Covered Service Providers

Service providers (and their affiliates and subcontractors) designated as "covered service providers" (CSPs) are required to make the mandatory disclosures. Covered services are the following:

- Services provided as a fiduciary either directly to the plan or to an investment vehicle holding plan assets, such as a mutual fund, or services provided as a registered investment adviser.
- Record keeping and brokerage services provided to participant-directed plans, if a designated investment alternative will be made available in connection with those services. A designated investment alternative is an investment option that a plan makes available, commonly on a menu of other designated investment alternatives
- Other services if the provider receives "indirect" compensation (compensation from a source other than the plan or plan sponsor)

Some service providers may not be aware that they have a disclosure obligation because they do not know that they are receiving indirect compensation. For example, under some arrangements, an account (sometimes called an ERISA account) will be used to hold 12b-1 or other revenue sharing directed to the account by the broker. Amounts in this account will be used to pay plan expenses for legal, accounting, and other services. If the plan sponsor is paying for these services, either directly out of the account or by paying providers (and being subsequently reimbursed from the account), these providers are receiving indirect compensation and have a disclosure obligation. I am aware of accounting and law firms that solve this problem by making the disclosures whether or not they are paid indirect compensation.

C. Information that Covered Service Providers Must Provide

Covered service providers must provide the following general types of information:

1. **Description of the services provided.** A CSP must describe the services to be provided under the contract or arrangement by the provider and any of its affiliates and subcontractors.
2. **Status as ERISA fiduciary or registered investment adviser.** This is great news for plan sponsors because now service providers must actually disclose whether they are acting in a fiduciary capacity.[68]

[68] Even with this disclosure, a plan sponsor's work is not done. Is this provider assuming full discretionary authority for making plan investments? Is it limiting its

3. **Disclosure of compensation.** This information must include how fees are paid and whether the fee is received directly from the plan or indirectly from a source other than the plan or the plan sponsor. Indirect fees are payments to the service provider from mutual funds or their managers or affiliates. CSPs must also disclose fees among related parties and their manner of receipt—that is, whether the fees are billed to the plan or automatically deducted from plan assets. The disclosure must describe any incentive compensation paid among the service provider, subcontractor, or affiliate if it is paid on a transaction basis and reduces the net value of the investment. Transaction-basis revenue includes commissions, soft dollars, or other incentive compensation.
4. **Termination charges.** The CSP must describe any compensation it reasonably expects to receive when the agreement or arrangement is terminated and how any prepaid amounts will be calculated and refunded.
5. **Record-keeping services.** Providers of record keeping services must give a description of those services and what they will be paid.
6. **Investment contract fiduciary service disclosures.** Providers of fiduciary services to a mutual fund, investment contract, or entity in which the plan is directly invested must make disclosures unless the broker or recordkeeper makes them.

D. Timing of Disclosures

The rules also require that disclosures be provided reasonably in advance of when a contract is entered into, extended, or renewed.[69] The "reasonably in advance" requirement is not clarified in the rules or in any subsequent guidance to date. Plan sponsors should consider how much time it would take to evaluate the new, extended, or renewed arrangement, taking into consideration the time needed for due diligence, including reference checks, benchmarking, comparison-shopping with other vendors, and other tasks. It's safe to say a disclosure made on Tuesday and an agreement signed on Wednesday is not a disclosure made reasonably in advance.

Pointer: Plan sponsors should keep a list of contract renewal dates and notify vendors in advance so they can provide the disclosures with enough time for the plan sponsor to consider the adequacy of the disclosures and the reasonableness of the arrangement.

---

responsibility to presenting a fund lineup for approval by the plan sponsor? What exactly is it doing in its fiduciary capacity?

[69] Labor Department Reg. Sec. 2550.408b-2(c)(v).

CSPs are also required to update annual disclosures before the next annual due date when they change a previously made disclosure. These changes must be disclosed within sixty days after the service provider becomes aware of the change.[70] Because plan sponsors are often not in a position to know when a change has been made, they should obligate the provider in its service agreement to give the notice. Another approach is to ask in writing the provider if any changes have occurred during the year that require disclosure. The update requirement does not apply to changes in investment information, which may be communicated annually regardless of when they become effective during the year.[71]

E. When a CSP Fails to Provide Disclosures

Covered service providers have a duty to provide information, and plan sponsors have a duty to obtain information. There may be errors in the information provided, omissions of information, or outright noncooperation in providing the information.

If a CSP fails to provide a disclosure to the plan sponsor (responsible plan fiduciary), the contract is de facto unreasonable, and a prohibited transaction results. The penalty to the service provider for a prohibited transaction is 15 percent nondeductible excise tax on the "amount involved."[72]

Plan sponsors may also be required to pay a prohibited transaction excise tax. However, the new rules provide a path for plan sponsors to avoid having the prohibited transaction rules applied to them. If a plan sponsor does not receive a disclosure, it can send the CSP a request for the disclosure. If the provider does not or refuses to provide the disclosure, the sponsor will not be subject to the tax if, within a certain period, it does the following:

- Notifies the Labor Department of the CSP's reporting failure. This notification can be accomplished electronically or via mail by visiting the Labor Department's website, which provides a link for the electronic filing and a printer friendly notice.[73]
- Fires the covered service provider.[74]

---

[70] Labor Department Reg. Sec. 2550.408b-2(c)(vi).

[71] Labor Department Reg. Sec. 2550.408b-2(c)(vi).

[72] Code Sec. 4975.

[73] http://www.dol.gov/ebsa/regs/feedisclosurefailurenotice.html.

[74] Labor Department Reg. Sec. 2550.408b-2(c)(ix).

POINTER: No prohibited transaction results if a service provider error was made in good faith and with reasonable diligence and the service provider remedies the error within thirty days of the time it discovers it.

In addition to the excise-tax consequences of a prohibited transaction, the transaction must be "corrected." Under IRS rules, this means the transaction must be undone or unwound so that the plan is put in the position it would have been had the transaction not occurred. In practical terms, the IRS could require the service provider to return all the fees it has earned under the plan agreement. Some commentators have suggested that the remedy is just simply providing the disclosure. No guidance has been issued to date on this point.

F. A Brief Checklist for Handling CSP Disclosures

Action	Reason
Appoint responsible plan fiduciary.	Someone needs to be in charge—in fact the disclosure rules requires it.
Create list of covered service providers.	The plan sponsor needs to know who is required to give it the disclosure.
Establish calendar of renewal dates for all service provider agreements.	The plan sponsor must know when agreements renew or terminate in the name of good plan management.
Establish calendar of annual disclosure dates for CSPs.	The plan sponsor must know when during the year a particular service provider is required to give you notice.
Send written notices to CSPs in advance of annual disclosure date.	This encourages the CSP to provide a timely disclosure and provides you with a record of your active management of the plan.
Timely evaluate all disclosures to determine whether informational requirements are met.	The plan sponsor can't know if disclosure information is missing if it hasn't read the disclosure.

Take steps to notify a CSP when there is no disclosure by the CSP or it is inadequate.	The provider owes the plan sponsor information. If the provider is not giving it to the sponsor, the sponsor must tell it!
Notify Labor Department if complete failure to disclose.	The plan sponsor does not want to pay excise taxes, does it?
Fire CSP if complete failure to disclose.	The plan sponsor does not want to pay excise taxes, does it?
Hire qualified independent adviser if necessary.	The reason is the same as hiring a mechanic to fix your car. If you don't know how to fix your car or don't have the time, you hire a mechanic that does.

G. Evaluating Service Provider Disclosures/Determining whether an Arrangement Is Reasonable

Once the plan sponsor has all the mandatory disclosures it can begin to decide if the arrangement is reasonable. The size of the plan sponsor and other factors dictates how the reasonableness evaluation will be done.

POINTER: Plan sponsors and their responsible fiduciaries must recognize that their brokers (sometimes called investment consultants), mutual fund bundled providers, and other providers are not disinterested parties to this process. Benchmarking reports from these sources should be looked at skeptically.

The plan sponsor must document the reasonableness of the arrangement in an evaluation that covers the following points:

1. **Knowing what other vendors are charging**. It is not possible for a plan sponsor to know whether they are paying a reasonable or market price if they do not know what other providers are charging similar plans. To get at this pricing, plan sponsors can use a process called benchmarking. With proper benchmarking, a plan sponsor looks at plans that are similar in participant account balances, participant accounts and assets, and other characteristics. It is truly a useless exercise to compare expenses in a plan with $5 million in assets with a plan with $25 million in assets. An apples to apples comparison is what the plan sponsor needs.

There are two basic approaches to benchmarking:

- *Plan sponsor does the research.* This may include talking with other plan sponsors willing to share their information and researching and reviewing trade industry articles about products and fees and related services, including employer satisfaction surveys. Such a strategy could include working with the plan's current vendor to obtain this information. It must be remembered they may not be disinterested.
- *Plan sponsor hires a consultant* who can advise you on fees and vendor alternatives and, importantly, knows the market. The consultant will have or obtain information about available products. A consultant's knowledge, acquired by working with other clients, can provide you highly useful information about vendors and their pricing. This process may lead to a request for information or to a request for a proposal, which is discussed in detail in the next chapter.

POINTER: Plan sponsors should consider hiring an independent consultant or adviser for this process, especially with the disclosure rules throwing very specific burdens on them.

The independence of any benchmarking is critical. I have seen situations where the provider "on behalf of" the employer requested the benchmarking from an independent service. The provider then controlled the assumptions that were used to benchmark. It was no surprise when the benchmarking showed the provider's fees in a favorable light even though it was clear to us that the provider's fees were excessive. I am also aware of benchmarking studies by major providers that use data from only their own clients. This type of benchmarking is useless. Benchmarking is discussed in more detail in the next section.

2. **Quality of services**. Quality of services is important, and going with the lowest cost provider may be the biggest mistake a plan sponsor can make. The plan sponsor's selection of a competent firm with significant experience in auditing employee-benefit plans is absolutely critical because a poor audit can cost you penalties, interest, and professional fees. Plan sponsors can be penny-wise and pound-foolish when it comes to employee-benefit plans.

POINTER: The lowest cost provider is not necessarily the best choice. Prudent decision-making may result in the selection of a service provider that charges more but provides greater value than someone charging less.

H. How to Approach Benchmarking

In determining fee reasonableness a plan sponsor has three tools: (1) benchmarking; (2) requests for information; and (3) requests for proposals. We look at benchmarking in this section and the other two tools in the next.

Technology has allowed for us to collect and analyze large amounts of data. Benchmarking utilizes this technology to correlate and compare plan data. Many rely on benchmarking for determining fee reasonableness. While this reliance is not totally misplaced, it is absolutely necessary for plan sponsors to understand the limitations of benchmarking and what factors to consider and questions to ask when requesting and then using a benchmarking report.

- Is the benchmarking provided by a completely *independent entity* that has nothing to gain or lose from what is in the report? If not, the report has to be looked at with skepticism.

Pointer: A report provided by the incumbent platform provider should not be given much credence.

- Does the report compare the plan against similar plans by plan assets, number of participants, company industry, plan type, plan features such as auto-enrollment, existence of matching contributions, percentage of plan assets in indexed funds and in managed funds, and other plan features?

Pointer: If a report does not have the characteristics described in the above bullet, it cannot be considered reliable.

- Is the database used to produce the report current, accurate, and extensive enough to produce a benchmarking comparison that can be trusted? As mentioned in the previous section a benchmarking that includes only the plans of one service provider is worthless in terms of producing any useful insights into market costs.
- In reviewing the benchmarking report, is the plan sponsor considering the quality of the services provided to the plan? Remember, a plan sponsor is under no obligation to hire the lowest-cost provider when a higher-cost provider is offering the plan more value.

POINTER: Any benchmarking report, even the best of them, is going to be somewhat dated and will not reflect the current market value of fees on the date it is provided. Benchmarking is a blunt instrument not a precision measuring tool.

POINTER: Although a benchmarking report can be used to leverage lower fees from a current provider or a new one, it does not create the leverage a request for proposal (RFP) or even a request for information (RFI) does.

It is not unreasonable to benchmark annually as benchmarking can be done inexpensively. If the plan sponsor does not take an annual approach, follow best practices and order a benchmarking after significant change to the plan or at least every three to five years.

I. RFPs and RFIs

The advantage of a request for proposal (RFP) or request for information (RFI) process is that it brings vendors to the table with real numbers against real competitors who are motivated to win the plan sponsor's business. Neither process will be successful, however, unless it is structured and coordinated. Many plan sponsors do not have the expertise or training to run the process, and in those cases, a consultant is brought in to run the process from beginning to end.

In general a well-conducted RFP process has the following benefits:

- It puts providers on notice that the plan is looking for providers in a competitive process.
- It requires the plan sponsor to specify its requirements—what it is looking for in a way that is intended to provide apple-to-apple comparisons of vendor proposals.
- It allows for wide distribution and response.
- It encourages providers to respond with information in a factual and systematic way.
- Following a structured process results in an impartial and reasoned result.

The RFI process is much less formal than the RFP process. The consultant, without naming the plan sponsor as his or her client, provides vendors basic information about the plan and in return receives informal quotes from the vendors on their range of fees for the plan. Often this process results in the plan sponsor going forward with an RFP.

Pointer: I have seen plan vendors offer significant adjustments based on an RFI request alone. It leaves one to wonder what else is being left on the table. What is under the table is discovered with an RFP.

J. Interest from Float

When distributions are made from a 401(k) or 403(b) plan or payments are made to service providers from the plan, funds for these disbursements are transferred from the plan to an omnibus account of the financial institution (custodian, trustee) from which checks are cut for the disbursement. Between the times the amounts are transferred to the omnibus account and the disbursements are made, the financial institution earns interest on the amount. This interest is not normally credited back to the plan. Rather, it is considered additional compensation paid to the financial institution.

If a financial institution earns interest on the float, the institution must disclose the fact to the plan sponsor, and the plan sponsor must consider whether that interest, together with other fees for custody, record keeping, and the like, are in the aggregate reasonable.

Pointer: If the plan sponsor cannot tell from its provider agreements or disclosures whether float income is part of the provider's compensation, it must inquire.

CHAPTER 8

Hiring a Plan Auditor

ERISA requires that plans of a certain size be audited by an independent certified public accountant and that the accountant's report to be submitted with the plan's annual return (Form 5500). This chapter discusses those rules and provides guidelines for selecting an auditor to prepare what is called the independent qualified plan audit report, or IQPA.

A. Timing and Purpose of the IQPA

Generally, federal law requires that employee-benefit plans with a hundred or more participants have an audit as part of their obligation in filing an annual return/report (Form 5500 series). Independent audits of employee-benefit plan financial statements are an important accountability mechanism. If the plan is required to have an audit, it is the plan sponsor's duty to hire an independent qualified public accountant and to ensure that the plan has a quality audit in accordance with ERISA and Department Labor requirements.

A quality audit helps protect the assets and the financial integrity of plan and helps the plan sponsor determine whether the necessary funds will be available to pay retirement benefits to its employees. The higher the quality of a plan's financial statement audit, the more reliable is the information used to manage and administer the plan. A quality audit also will help the plan sponsor carry out its legal responsibility to file a complete and accurate annual return/report for the plan each year. Thus, the selection of an experienced and reliable auditor is very important.

ERISA holds the plan sponsor responsible for ensuring that plan financial statements are properly audited in accordance with generally accepted auditing standards (GAAS).

B. How to Select an Auditor

The selection of a plan auditor is a high priority and requires care during every phase of the selection process. The Labor Department's Employee Benefits Security Administration (EBSA) has published a booklet titled *Selecting an Auditor for Your Employee Benefit Plan.*[75] Its key points are briefly summarized in the table below:

Key Point	Requirement
License or certification	ERISA requires that an auditor be licensed or certified as a public accountant by a state regulatory authority.
Auditor independence	Auditors should not have financial interests in the plan or in the plan sponsor that would affect their ability to render an objective, unbiased opinion about the financial condition of the plan. For example, a financial interest in the plan sponsor is disqualifying, as would the maintenance by the auditor of the plan's financial records; i.e. the auditor cannot be in a position of checking its own work.
Experience	A common deficiency in plan audit reports is the failure of the auditor to perform tests in areas unique to employee-benefit plan audits. The more training and experience the auditor has, the better the audit will be.

[75] http://www.dol.gov/ebsa/publications/selectinganauditor.html

Checking references, licenses, and experience	A best practice is to request confirmation of licenses and to inquire about the experience of auditor staff and the number of employee-benefit plan audits the auditor has performed.
Engagement letters	All auditor engagements should be subject to an engagement letter or agreement spelling out the work to be performed and the deliverables.

The plan sponsor may wish to engage in an RFP process for the audit. The American Institute of Certified Public Accountants (AICPA) website is an excellent resource for finding member audit firms subscribing to its audit standards and for information on how to conduct an RFP.[76] The Labor Department also provides useful tips at its website.[77]

C. What an IQPA Does and Doesn't Do

In general the audit will consider the following areas:

- Have plan assets have been fairly valued?
- Are plan obligations properly stated and described?
- Are contributions to the plan timely?
- Were benefit payments made in accordance with plan terms?
- Are participant accounts properly stated?
- Were issues identified that may impact the plan's tax status?
- Were prohibited transactions properly identified?

An IQPA does not consider issues relating to the general governance of your plan, the oversight of plan service providers, the reasonableness of fees, whether the plan documentation is up to date, whether plan investments are appropriate, or whether plan participants have been properly notified under the various notification requirements. For these services plan sponsors need other professionals such as investment advisers, plan governance consultants, attorneys and others.

[76] http://www.aicpa.org/Pages/default.aspx.

[77] See "Selecting an Auditor for Your Plan," US Department of Labor website, http://www.dol.gov/ebsa/publications/selectinganauditor.html.

D. Labor Department Penalties

The plan sponsor faces a significant amount of risk associated with deficiencies or missing audits of your ERISA plans. Recent Labor Department studies of audit quality found deficiencies in plan audits. The Labor Department has responded with new enforcement strategies for audit deficiencies. The penalties for audit failures can be substantial. The Labor Department can assess penalties of up to $1,100 a day, capped at $50,000 per annual report filing, where the required auditor's report is missing or deficient. A few years ago the Labor Department established a "forgiveness" program for delinquent filings. This program is discussed in chapter 15.

CHAPTER 9

Managing Plan Documentation

Every plan sponsor manages its plan under a set of plan documents that govern the administration of the plan and that must be followed and kept up to date. This chapter discusses critical points in the management of that documentation.

A. Familiarity with Plan Documents

The plan sponsor must read and understand the basic plan documents. Documents used in plan administration (e.g., SPDs and forms) must be consistent with operative plan provisions, and the plan sponsor must be diligent in ferreting out inconsistencies, inaccuracies, and ambiguities. The plan sponsor generally is responsible for the interpretation and administration of the plan documents, although these responsibilities may be delegated to others.[78]

POINTER: Newly appointed plan fiduciaries should be provided with training that includes their general obligations under law and specific obligations under the plan documents. They should from the beginning become familiar with plan documents.

---

[78] As defined in ERISA Sec. 3(16).

B. Legal Compliance

The plan sponsor must ensure that plan documents and operations are in full compliance with all applicable laws. As a result, the sponsor must keep abreast of the changes in the law and in regulatory guidance. Periodically, the sponsor should consult with legal counsel and its document providers regarding the conformity of the plan document and its operation with the law.

C. Individually Designed and Preapproved Plan Documents

Plan sponsors of 401(k) plans who adopt individually designed plan documents must take special care in maintaining the plan's tax-qualified status under the Internal Revenue Code. The plan should be reviewed annually to determine whether it must be amended to maintain its qualification. It is good practice, although not legally required, to obtain a determination letter from the IRS on the tax qualification of the plan when it is initially established and when significant amendments are made. There is currently no procedure for obtaining a determination letter for individually-designed 403(b) plans, although the IRS does have a program for pre-approved prototype 403(b) plans, discussed in the next paragraph.

If the sponsor uses IRS preapproved prototype documents, it will be precluded from getting an individual determination letter from the IRS if the document used is a "standardized" document. If the document is "non-standardized," the IRS allows the plan sponsor to either rely on the preapproved document or to apply for an individual determination letter. When a plan sponsor substantially modifies a standardized or non-standardized document, the plan will be treated as individually designed. If the sponsor is considering modification of these types of documents, it should consult ERISA counsel for advice.

Plan sponsors may also use volume submitter documents that are also IRS pre-approved. These documents allow sponsors ability to include special provisions that it could not include in any type of prototype document. In any case it is important to remember IRS pre-approved plans will have an opinion letter from the IRS stating that it approves only of the form of the documentation. The IRS does not express an opinion or determination on the tax-qualified status of the plan as adopted by particular plan sponsors. For this reason many employee benefit attorneys recommend that plan sponsors adopt a form of documentation allowing them to apply for and receive an IRS determination letter as to their plan's tax-qualified status.

D. Plan Amendments

From time to time, plan amendments may be necessary either because the law requires it or because of a decision to make changes in the design of the plan. These changes should be reviewed with appropriate plan service providers, including actuaries, consultants, accountants, and legal counsel, and amendments should be prepared or reviewed by counsel.

Pointer: The plan sponsor should have an annual review of plan amendment status. In addition, reports to a delegating fiduciary, such as a board of directors, should specify whether all required amendments have been made to the plan.

E. Communicating with Service Providers and Participants

The plan sponsor must communicate changes in the plan to the appropriate plan stakeholders. For example, if there is a change in the plan's definition of compensation, then payroll and the TPA should be notified. Also, the change must be reflected in the plan's summary plan description (a document that is required to be provided to all participants and beneficiaries). Informal communications to explain the amendment to participants should be considered too. This is particularly important if the change might be considered a take-away.

F. Avoiding De Novo Standard of Review

When a dispute over a plan sponsor's interpretation of a plan provision goes to court, the court can look at the reasonableness of the sponsor's interpretation in one of two ways. Under the "de novo" standard of review, it looks at the interpretation with fresh eyes and asks the question, "What is my reasonable interpretation?" In other words, the court has a great deal of latitude in deciding whether the sponsor's interpretation is right. A plan sponsor therefore, does not want a de novo standard of review—it's just too easy for the court to second-guess.

Courts apply the de novo standard when the plan document does not explicitly say the plan sponsor or plan administrator has the authority to interpret the plan. Now you may be completely lost, but bear with me. To interpret a plan provision means to supply meaning to plan language that is not clear or is ambiguous.

The second way courts look at plan sponsor interpretations of plan provisions is to ask the question "Is the plan sponsor's interpretation totally without merit or any reason?" If the interpretation is not totally unreasonable, the court will side with the plan sponsor. Essentially the court is saying even though it might disagree with the sponsor, it will let the decision stand.

Pointer: Most employee-benefit plans contain explicit language that states the sponsor interprets the plan, so for most plan sponsors, their plans avoid a de novo standard of review. The only way the plan sponsor can know the situation is to read the plan or ask its attorney to do it. Ideal language might read as follows: "The plan administrator shall have the sole discretion to construe and interpret the plan, including, but not limited to the determination of eligibility and benefits." For plans without this language, the plan sponsor should consider adding it or something like it. It's best to talk to an attorney about the best language for this purpose.

CHAPTER 10

Plan Administration

This chapter covers aspects of a plan's administration. As discussed in chapter 1, these tasks are normally the direct responsibility of the third-party administrator, or TPA. The plan administrator or plan sponsor has overall responsibility for reviewing the TPA's output (reports that may be provided on a monthly, quarterly, and annual basis) and for overseeing the performance of the TPA.

A. Administration Tasks

The table below summarizes these tasks[79] and the extent of the division of responsibilities between plan administrator and TPA.

Task	Assignment of Responsibility
Coverage testing. Plans must cover a minimum percentage of eligible employees under the requirements of the Internal Revenue Code.	• TPA does the testing. • Plan sponsor reviews.

[79] Code Sec. 410.

Discrimination testing. In 401(k) plan parlance, this generally refers to the ADP and ACP tests of discrimination in elective salary-deferral and matching contributions, although it can also refer to discrimination testing on compensation used for determining benefits.[80]	• TPA performs these tests based on data provided by plan sponsor. • Plan sponsor must understand and review this testing for accuracy and completeness.
Allocations of contributions to participant accounts.	• TPA does the work. • Plan sponsor must understand and review these calculations.
Vesting determinations.	• TPA determines the vested percentage of individual participant accounts. • Plan sponsor reviews.
Participant loans.	• TPA is responsible for granting loans based on the plan's provisions and associated participant loan policy.[81] • Plan sponsor must understand the loan policy and assure itself that the TPA is following the terms of the plan and the loan policy.
Qualified domestic relations orders (QDROs).	• Authority to determine whether a domestic relations order is "qualified"[82] usually rests with the plan administrator but sometimes can be found with the TPA. • Plan sponsor is responsible for establishing a QDRO procedure and for ensuring that it is followed.

[80] Code Secs. 401(k) and 401(m).

[81] Plans are required to have a participant loan policy setting forth rates of interest and default rules, among other things.

Distributions from plan. These normally include in-service, termination of employment, hardship, retirement, and beneficiary distributions.	• TPA generally administers these distributions. • Plan administrator has final sign-off authority.
Top-heavy determinations.[83] A top-heavy determination may result in accelerated vesting and is likely to require additional minimum contributions.	• TPA is normally responsible, using account balance and other information. • Plan sponsor reviews and takes appropriate action.
Participant claims procedures. Every plan must have a claims procedure, which the plan administrator is responsible for administering	• Plan sponsor normally has this responsibility.
Participant notices. 401(k) plans and 403(b) plans are subject to any of a number of requirements regarding notice to participants of their rights under the plan, including quarterly and annual notices regarding investment rights, plan and account and expenses, and various safe-harbor notices.	• Plan sponsor is responsible for the delivery of these notices. • TPA, recordkeeper or bundled service provider may be the agent for delivery.

[82] See Code Sec. 414(p).

[83] ERISA Section 403(b) plans are not subject to the top-heavy rules. Generally the top-heavy rules come into play when the account balances of certain "key employees" comprise more than 60 percent of all plan account balances.

Reporting to the government.	• TPA prepares the returns for the review, signature, and filing by the plan administrator. • Plan sponsor is responsible for filing annual returns (Form 5500) under penalty of perjury. POINTER: The plan administrator must review the return carefully for accuracy and completeness. The plan sponsor must review the return skeptically and with an eye for detail. If an auditor's report has been provided, it must be reviewed for any misstatements of fact on which the auditor's conclusions are based This review should take into consideration whether the auditor tested: (1) the fair valuation of plan assets, (2) timeliness of contributions, (3) whether benefits were distributed in accordance with the terms of the plan, and (4) whether there were any prohibited transactions.
Request by participants for plan documents and benefit information. Participants also have the right to request the delivery of benefit calculations.	• Plan sponsor has the responsibility to deliver documents. • Responsibilities may be delegated to others, including the TPA.
Summary plan description (SPD). The typical plan will have an SPD drafted by an attorney, the bundled service provider, TPA, or other provider.	• Plan sponsor has the obligation of reviewing the SPD against the plan document for consistency and updating it either by amending it or supplementing it with a summary of material modifications (SMM). • Plan sponsor also has responsibility for making sure participants receive the SPD.

Fidelity bond. Federal law requires a fidelity bond for the protection of the plan against the theft or loss of plan funds by persons handling plan assets.[84]	• Plan sponsor has the responsibility. • Service providers handling the plan's money also need one.
Communication with service providers and finance and human resources staff.	• The important players involved in plan administration must be kept in the loop, and generally it is the plan administrator that has the critical role in this regard.

B. Responsibility for Interpreting the Plan

Most plan documents leave responsibility for interpreting plan provisions to the plan administrator (in many cases the plan sponsor). Sometimes the TPA will run into a plan provision that is susceptible to alternative interpretations. The TPA then will look to the plan administrator to provide an interpretation. If the TPA is taking on this responsibility, either contractually or in practice, it will have fiduciary responsibility for the decisions it makes.

Pointer: A best practice when a question of plan interpretation arises is for the plan administrator to issue a "written plan administrator's order." Such an order is a written record that helps ensure consistency in the interpretation of the plan.

C. Responsibility for Performance of TPA and Other Plan Service Providers

The plan administrator is not responsible for the actual detail of the work performed by a TPA or other service providers. However, it does have responsibility for reviewing providers' performance. In addition to reviewing the output of plan service providers, such as the reports described in the table above, the administrator must evaluate whether the provider is performing up to expectations and in accordance with contractual agreements and industry standards. If action is warranted based on this review, the administrator must take it. Such an action might include replacing the service provider or adjusting its arrangements with the provider.

[84] ERISA Sec. 412.

D. Delinquent Remittance of Salary-Deferral Contributions by Plan Sponsor

Salary-deferral contributions must be made as soon as administratively practicable after they are deducted from pay, but no later than the fifteenth day after the end of the plan month in which they are deducted. The Labor Department has said that the fifteen-day rule is not a safe harbor and that it expects contributions to be deposited or transferred as soon as administratively feasible.

There is a special rule for plans of small employers with fewer than one hundred plan participants. If a small employer deposits salary-deferral contributions by the seventh business day following the withholding date, the Labor Department will consider the deposit to be timely and the employer will not be subject to sanctions for late deposits.

Pointer: The plan sponsor must take the "as soon as practicable" rule very seriously. No large plan sponsor should think it has until the last day possible to make the contribution. The better approach is to think three to five business days after the amount is deducted from payroll as the latest "safe" date for the contributions. If a plan sponsor has the capability of doing it more quickly than that, then it must.

E. Settlor versus Plan Administration Expenses

In its guidance, the Labor Department has addressed the issue of the payment of expenses by the plan that might be viewed as conferring a benefit on the plan sponsor. In general, expenses that relate to the plan sponsor's decision to sponsor, change a benefit feature, or terminate a plan cannot be paid from plan assets. Only expenses for the plan's administration may be paid from plan assets. Legal advice should be sought when it is questionable whether the expense is settlor or plan-related.

CHAPTER 11

Plan Investments

There is no doubt that plan investment is the area of plan activity that receives the most attention from plan sponsors and their advisors. So let's turn to it now. As a general rule, a plan sponsor's board of directors delegates investment authority to trustees (either individuals or an institution such as a bank or trust company), a committee, or an investment manager. Most 401(k) and virtually all 403(b) plans allow participants to direct their investments in accounts from a menu of mutual funds selected by the plan sponsor or one of its delegates described in the preceding chapter. In fact, many 403(b) plans allow participants to pick among the funds of sometimes several vendors, not just a pre-set menu of mutual fund investment options from one vendor.[85]

Most plan sponsors who are professionally advised will build plan investments around an investment policy statement, or IPS. Although the creation of an IPS is not legally required, it is a best-practice way to provide for the selection and monitoring of plan investments.

[85] There is a trend away from this type of 403(b) arrangement to 401(k) type arrangements. Ease of administration and potential reduced costs are two reasons for this development.

A. Key Elements of an Investment Policy Statement

An IPS describes investment objectives, establishes the frequency of investment performance monitoring, and establishes the frequency with which investment performance is monitored. An IPS also assigns responsibility for the monitoring and review and modification of the policy itself. The IPS includes the following elements:

- An evaluation of the specific needs of the plan and its participants
- Recitation of the investment objectives and goals of the plan
- Description of the duties and responsibilities of all parties involved
- Description of the due diligence criteria for selecting investment options for the plan
- Description of the classes and styles of investment permitted
- Standards and bench marks of investment performance used for comparison
- Policies and procedures related to hiring, monitoring, and replacing investment managers and funds
- Policies related to the prevention of prohibited transactions
- Whether the plan permits participant-directed investments under ERISA section 404(c)

POINTER: A well-crafted IPS will be principles-based and provide sufficient guidance for plan fiduciary decisions without creating so many detailed rules that fiduciaries ending up tripping over them.

B. Delegation of Responsibilities

Fiduciaries are generally not liable for a breach of duty if that duty has been specifically delegated to another fiduciary. This defense applies only if the plan document specifically authorizes the delegation.

C. Qualifications of the Investment Fiduciary

Reasonable prudence must be exercised in delegating responsibilities. The persons selected must satisfy ERISA qualifications and be capable of adequately discharging the responsibilities delegated. Before selecting the investment manager, fiduciaries must investigate and document the qualifications and backgrounds of the candidates.

D. Trustees

Trustee responsibilities should be clearly delineated in the trust agreement, and any carve-outs for investment discretion in an investment manager, investment committee, or other fiduciary must be clearly stated.

E. Investment Managers

Fiduciaries should delegate responsibility for the management or control of plan assets only to an investment manager who is a registered investment adviser, a bank, or a qualified insurance company. These are the people that make the individual investment decisions and do not merely offer investment advice.

POINTER: A written acknowledgment of the investment manager's status as an ERISA fiduciary should be obtained to provide plan sponsor fiduciaries with the greatest protection from liability.

F. Monitoring

Appointing fiduciaries must oversee and monitor investment managers and advisers. An active and comprehensive monitoring program should be implemented to evaluate the performance of the appointee and the appropriateness of continuing that delegation as an investment fiduciary. Depending on the circumstances, this evaluation can occur through formal periodic reviews, or day-to-day contact, and communication.

G. Documenting Investment Decisions and Monitoring

It's critical to create documents that serve as evidence of a deliberative process in selecting investment fiduciaries and also regarding particular investment decisions. A record of monitoring and analyzing the continued suitability of plan investments in light of market conditions should be maintained. Investment performance must be periodically evaluated against the IPS.

H. Prohibited Transactions and Special Situations

Investment fiduciaries must be aware of federal laws that may preclude particular plan investments or result in undesirable tax costs. For example, a loan by the plan to the plan sponsor subjects the plan sponsor to punitive excise taxes, unless otherwise exempted. Plan investments that are debt financed are subject to very high trust income tax rates under section 512 of the Internal Revenue Code. Also, plans may not make foreign investment unless what is called the indicia of ownership is within the jurisdiction of the federal courts.[86] Each of these limitations should be considered in the IPS and communicated to responsible investment fiduciaries.

I. Limited Partnership and Other Alternative Forms of Investment[87]

Investments in limited partnerships, hedge funds and other hard-to-value assets invite special scrutiny because of the risk of prohibited transactions and the hard-to-value nature of these investments. For example, under certain conditions the underlying assets of an investment in a limited partnership may be considered plan assets. This in turn means that routine transactions involving the partnership and its managers and others would be prohibited.[88] Because these investments are often hard-to-value, it is often difficult for plan fiduciaries to determine the true value of the investment for plan reporting and participant distribution purposes.

J. 1940 Act Hedge Fund Investments

Recently there has been an interest in, or at least an advocacy by some of, 401(k) and 403(b) plan investments in "40 Act Hedge Funds." High fees and the need for plan liquidity may not make these funds the best investment alternative for 401(k) or 403(b) plans. These investments should be looked at critically by responsible plan fiduciaries before investing in them.

[86] 29 CFR 2550.404b-1.

[87] These investments are not permitted in Section 403(b) plans.

[88] Labor Department Reg. 29 CFR 2510.3-101 sets forth rules for determining whether the underlying assets are plan assets.

CHAPTER 12

Participant Directed Investments

Perhaps no area of 401(k) and 403(b) plan responsibility has caused more confusion or generated more misinformation than participant-directed investments. Mutual fund and other institutional salespeople have sold the participant-directed option to employers as a method of fully escaping liability for investment decisions. This is not true. Others have dismissed the approach because the obstacles to fully satisfying the requirements of ERISA for participant directed investments under ERISA section 404(c) are, in their opinion, so formidable they cannot be overcome—so why try? The reality lies somewhere in the middle. In fact most plan sponsors do allow participants to direct the investments in their accounts.[89]

The advantages to plan sponsors offering participant-directed investment of plan accounts under 404(c) are these:

- Participants have the opportunity to tailor their investments to their particular needs, and the plan sponsor is not involved in participant investment decisions.

[89] This despite convincing evidence that professional investment of plan assets in pension plans yields greater year-to-year returns than do investments in participant-directed plans. See, for example a Towers Watson study showing that defined-benefit plan investments consistently outperform 401(k) participant-directed investments. See http://www.towerswatson.com/en/Press/2013/05/Defined-Benefit-Plans-Outperformed-401k-Plans-During-2011-by-Largest-Margin-Since-Mid-1990s.

- The plan sponsor will have an *affirmative defense* to a claim by a participant that the sponsor is responsible for losses in the participant's account, as long as it has satisfied the requirements of section 404(c) and related regulations. This is not a bad thing, but freedom from liability for the participant's investment decisions is not guaranteed.[90]

Participant-directed investments are not required. Nor is compliance with section 404(c) required. But if a plan sponsor permits participant-directed investments but it does not elect a 404(c) design, plan fiduciaries may be liable for damages resulting from participants' investment losses.

POINTER: The plan sponsor must affirmatively elect the 404(c) design by communicating the intention in writing to participants and by indicating this intention on the annual return (Form 5500).

POINTER: ERISA section 404(c) cannot be viewed in isolation. Compliance with it is closely interwoven with the fee disclosure rules discussed in chapter 7 and the qualified default investment or QDIA rules for plan sponsors who elect this investment option discussed later in this chapter.

Plan sponsors that are not committed to strict compliance with these rules should eliminate participant directed investment and hire an investment manager to invest plan money. The rest of this chapter describes the design for plan sponsors that want to have 404(c) protection.

A. What Is a Participant-Directed Investment under 404(c)?

Section 401(k) and more recently section 403(b) plans generally offer a limited menu of mutual fund as investment choice for participants. The plan sponsor, either with or without the advice of an investment advisor, or an investment manager chooses the investment lineup. Sometimes these plans will offer a brokerage window through which participants can elect investments in individual stocks and bonds. Brokerage windows are also available to participants in 403(b) plans, but participants may only invest in annuity-type and mutual fund investments.

[90] There is a division of authority on whether 404(c) relieves a plan sponsor from liability for selecting the investment liability. The Labor Department continues to hold the position that it does not.

B. Opportunity to Exercise Meaningful Control is Critical

The essential rule of the ERISA section 404(c) regulations is that plans using it must provide participants the opportunity to exercise meaningful, independent control over the assets in their accounts. The facts of each case determine if control is independent. For example, the decision is not independent if the plan sponsor improperly influences the participant or conceals information or if the participant is legally incompetent. To ensure meaningful control, the participant must have the opportunity to:

- Choose from a broad range of investment options that allow diversification within a single option as well as among various options.
- Give investment instructions with a frequency that is appropriate in light of the market volatility of the investment option.
- Obtain sufficient information to make informed decisions.

C. Broad Range of Investment Options Must Be Offered

Participants must be able to choose from a broad range of investment options. This is defined as providing participants with the opportunity to affect returns on at least three investment options (core alternatives). The core alternative options must be diversified and must have materially different risk and return characteristics. Since each core alternative must itself be diversified, certain types of investment funds, such as employer stock, cannot qualify as a core alternative. The three core investment options might be a money-market fund, a bond fund, and an equity (stock) fund.

D. Restrictions on Investment Directions

The plan administrator may decline a participant's investment instructions if those directions would jeopardize the qualified status of the plan, are not in accordance with the provisions of the plan, or would cause a prohibited transaction. The plan administrator may also decline instructions that could cause a loss in excess of the participant's account balance or would create income taxable (unrelated business taxable income or UBTI) to the plan.

Reasonable restrictions on the frequency of investment may also be placed on participants. What is and what is not a reasonable frequency restriction is determined by the volatility of the investment. The following two methods can be used to judge whether a restriction is reasonable:

- Under the *three-month method,* core alternatives must allow participants to transfer to another core alternative not less frequently than once in any three-month period. Because of this requirement, certain types of investments that restrict or prohibit direct transfers cannot qualify as a core alternative whose terms provide that money transferred out of it may not be moved into it for more than a three month period. For example, a fixed-rate contract having such a restriction cannot be offered as a core alternative.
- Under the *volatile investment method,* participants must be given the opportunity to move from a more volatile investment option to (1) a less volatile option that is one of the core alternatives at least as often as a participant can transfer amounts out of a more volatile investment; or (2) an income-producing, low-risk, liquid option that holds transferred money until the opportunity becomes available for the money to be transferred into a core alternative.

E. Participant Investment Instructions

To qualify as a participant-directed account and thereby enable the plan fiduciary to receive the protection of ERISA section 404(c), the participant who owns the account must provide specific investment instructions. The participant must sign a written agreement directing how the assets are to be invested in the absence of specific direction. If a participant does not provide investment direction, the fiduciary may make a default investment on behalf of the participant. The Pension Protection Act of 2006 (PPA) provides fiduciaries the means of obtaining relief from liability for default investments. Plan sponsors now have the ability to offer participants a Qualified Default Investment Alternatives (QDIAs) described in the following section.

F. Qualified Default Investment Alternatives

Plan sponsors may gain additional protection from liability by offering a QDIA to participants who fail to direct the investment of their accounts. Typically, this feature is used with a plan that automatically defers employee salary (negative election).

A QDIA may be one of four investment alternatives: (1) an age- or retirement-based fund, such as a life cycle or target retirement date fund; (2) an option that allocates contributions among existing plan investment options based on an individual's age or retirement date; (3) a fund based on plan demographics to find an appropriate investment mix (e.g., a balanced fund); and (4) a capital preservation option that may be used for only the first 120 days in the event employees automatically enrolled decide to opt out of participating. Certain participant notification and other requirements must also be satisfied.

G. Information that Must Be Disclosed to Participants

To find that participants have meaningful control, sufficient information must be made available to them to permit informed investment decisions. This requirement applies to initial and ongoing investment decisions. The information in the following table may be provided in the summary plan description, enrollment package, or other notices.

Relevant Information	Description
Statement of intent to be 404(c) compliant	An explanation of the plan's intent to be an ERISA section 404(c) plan and that plan fiduciaries of an ERISA section 404(c) plan are relieved of liability for losses resulting from participants' investment decisions. This election should also be made on the plan's annual return each year.
Description of designated investment options	A description of all designated investment options, including a general description of the investment objectives, risks and returns characteristics, and information about the diversification of assets.
Identification of investment manager	Identification of any designated investment manager.
Explanation of investment instructions	An explanation of how a participant gives investment instructions; the limits and restrictions on giving instructions, such as information about withdrawal penalties and transfer restrictions; and restrictions concerning voting, tender, or similar rights.

Description of transaction fees and expenses	A description of transaction fees or expenses charged to the participant's account from the purchase or sale of an investment option.
Description of information available on request	A description that additional information is available on request, as well as the name, address, and phone number of the person or persons responsible for providing that information.
Description of confidentiality procedures	A description of procedures that keep participants' direction with respect to employer securities confidential, as well as identification information (such as the name, address, and phone number) of the plan fiduciary responsible for monitoring compliance with those procedures.
Prospectus	A prospectus must be given immediately before or after a participant's initial investment in an option that is subject to the Securities Act of 1933, such as mutual funds and insurance company registered products.
Description of voting, tender, and similar rights	Materials relating to voting, tender, or similar rights, including information describing the nature of the pass-through rights available under the plan, to the extent that these rights are passed through to participants. The plan fiduciary may designate another person to act on the fiduciary's behalf in providing required information.

POINTER: Many, if not all, of these disclosures, will be provided through plan service providers, such as the platform provider, recordkeeper, or TPA. The plan sponsor must make a determination that the disclosures are being handled properly.

H. Information that Must Be Provided upon Request

Relevant Information	Description
Annual operating expenses and costs of investments	A description of the operating expense of each investment option
Prospectuses, financial statements, and reports	Copies of prospectuses, financial statements, and reports, as well as any other information furnished to the plan relating to investment options
Listing of investment fund assets	A listing of assets that comprise the portfolio of an investment option, and the name of the issuer, term, and rate of return for fixed-rate investment contracts
Total value of share information	Information concerning the total value of shares or units in the investment options available to participants
Participant account values	Information concerning the value of shares or units in the investment options held in the participant's account

POINTER: The information described in the table above can normally be found on provider or fund websites.

I. Investments in Employer Stock[91]

Section 401(k) plans that want to permit participants to invest in employer stock under the participant directed account rules must satisfy the following conditions:

- The stock must be publicly traded on a recognized market, and trading volume must be sufficient for transactions to be executed promptly.
- Shareholder information must be provided; additionally, voting and similar rights must be passed through to participants.

[91] Obviously investments in a tax-exempt plan sponsor entity are not a consideration for participants in a 403(b) plan.

- Information relating to the purchase, holding, or sale of employer securities, as well as the exercise of voting rights, must be maintained in accordance with procedures designed to safeguard the confidentiality of such information, except to the extent necessary to comply with relevant federal and state laws.
- The plan must designate a fiduciary to be responsible for ensuring the confidentiality procedures mentioned above are being followed. Also, an outside, independent fiduciary must be appointed to carry out activities involving a potential for undue employer influence on participants with regard to exercising their shareholder rights.

If the employer stock fund fails to meet the above requirements (for example, the stock is not publicly traded), the plan may still obtain ERISA section 404(c) compliance for the other plan investments. Plan fiduciaries, however, would have no protection from liability for participants' investment directions to the employer stock fund.

POINTER: Offering employer stock in a 401(k) plan must be carefully considered. In the case of non-publicly traded companies, the valuation of shares is an ongoing proposition for purposes of determining distributions and annual reporting. For publicly traded corporations subject to the federal securities laws, the potential for conflict between fiduciary duty to the plan and insider trading rules is quite real and must be addressed in advance.

J. Brokerage Accounts

Brokerage accounts, sometimes called brokerage windows, permit 401(k) plan[92] participants to invest in individual securities or other investments the brokerage firm offers and are generally offered as an alterative to a designated lineup of mutual-fund type of investments.[93] In other words, an individual can buy and sell just as they would in a regular, taxable account. These accounts are offered as way to allow experienced participant-investors the greatest possible choice of investment return.

[92] Indvidual stocks and bonds, limited partnerships, real and personal property are *not* permissible investments for 403(b) plans. It is possible a brokerage window could offer investments in mutual funds not part of the basic investment menu but not likely.

[93] Some plans establish all participants in brokerage accounts, and the plan sponsor does not designate specific mutual-fund investments for participant investment. Plan sponsors should consult with benefit plan experts and legal counsel regarding the application of the participant fee and investment disclosures rules described in chapter 7.

Critics of brokerage accounts say they encourage participants to buy and sell frequently, which is contradictory to long-term savings. Other critics say unlimited choice may be confusing or intimidating. Plan sponsors whose plans contain this feature must establish a minimum level of oversight and the reasonableness of fees. This oversight does not extend to responsibility for individual participant investment decisions if the arrangement otherwise satisfies the participant-directed account rules under ERISA, as described in this chapter.

Brokerage windows are different from plans set up with f/b/o or "for the benefit of" accounts for all participants who then may invest their accounts in generally any investment that is made available under the plan's agreement with the broker. The Labor Department has expressed great skepticism about these accounts, viewing some of them as a subterfuge for avoiding the participant fee disclosure rules described in chapter 13. Get some advice from a benefits attorney if the plan maintains this type of arrangement or the plan sponsor is considering it.

K. Participant Investment Education versus Advice

For some time, advisors to plan sponsors have advised them to be careful about how they convey investment information to participants. If that information is considered too individualized, the plan sponsor or investment adviser or consultant will be considered to have rendered "investment advice," thus inviting fiduciary status under ERISA and related liability.

The best approach for avoiding this fate is to rely on Labor Department guidance describing what participant education is, the substance of which is repeated here. Another way to say this is when the plan sponsor provides only the information described below it is not providing investment advice.

Plan Information. This is information and materials that inform a participant about:

- The benefits of plan participation, the benefits of increasing plan contributions, the impact of preretirement withdrawals on retirement income, the terms of the plan, or the operation of the plan; or
- Investment alternatives under the plan (e.g., descriptions of investment objectives and philosophies, risk and return characteristics, historical return information, or related prospectuses).

General Financial and Investment Information. This is information anz materials that inform a participant or beneficiary about:

- General financial and investment concepts, such as risk and return, diversification, dollar cost averaging, compounded return, and tax deferred investment;
- Historic differences in rates of return between different asset classes (e.g., equities, bonds, or cash) based on standard market indices;
- Effects of inflation; (iv) estimating future retirement income needs;
- Determining investment time horizons; and
- Assessing risk tolerance.

Asset Allocation Models. This is information and materials (e.g., pie charts, graphs, or case studies) that provide a participant or beneficiary with models, available to all plan participants and beneficiaries, of asset allocation portfolios of hypothetical individuals with different time horizons and risk profiles, where:

- Such models are based on generally accepted investments theories that take into account the historic returns of different asset classes (e.g., equities, bonds, or cash) over defined periods of time;
- All material facts and assumptions on which such models are based (e.g., retirement ages, life expectancies, income levels, financial resources, replacement income ratios, inflation rates, and rates of return) accompany the models;
- To the extent that an asset allocation model identifies any specific investment alternative available under the plan, the model is accompanied by a statement indicating that other investment alternatives having similar risk and return characteristics may be available under the plan and identifying where information on those investment alternatives may be obtained; and
- The asset allocation models are accompanied by a statement indicating that, in applying particular asset allocation models to their individual situations, participants or beneficiaries should consider their other assets, income, and investments (e.g., equity in a home, IRA investments, savings accounts, and interests in other qualified and non-qualified plans) in addition to their interests in the plan.

Interactive Investment Materials. These materials may include questionnaires, worksheets, software, and similar materials which provide a participant or beneficiary the means to estimate future retirement income needs and assess the impact of different asset allocations on retirement income, where:

- The materials are based on generally accepted investment theories that take into account the historic returns of different asset classes (e.g., equities, bonds, or cash) over defined periods of time;

- There is an objective correlation between the asset allocations generated by the materials and the information and data supplied by the participant or beneficiary;
- All material facts and assumptions (e.g., retirement ages, life expectancies, income levels, financial resources, replacement income ratios, inflation rates, and rates of return) which may affect a participant's or beneficiary's assessment of the different asset allocations accompany the materials or are specified by the participant or beneficiary;
- To the extent that an asset allocation generated by the materials identifies any specific investment alternative available under the plan, the asset allocation is accompanied by a statement indicating that other investment alternatives having similar risk and return characteristics may be available under the plan and identifying where information on those investment alternatives may be obtained; and
- The materials either take into account or are accompanied by a statement indicating that, in applying particular asset allocations to their individual situations, participants or beneficiaries should consider their other assets, income, and investments (e.g., equity in a home, IRA investments, savings accounts, and interests in other qualified and non-qualified plans) in addition to their interests in the plan. [94]

L. Participant Investment Advice

Under ERISA a person is considered a fiduciary with respect to an employee-benefit plan to the extent that person "renders investment advice for a fee or other compensation, direct or indirect, with respect to any moneys or other property of such plan, or has any authority to do so." The Labor Department has a longstanding rule (discussed in chapter 1) describing the circumstances under which a person will be considered to be rendering "investment advice."

A person will be considered to be rendering "investment advice" to a participant or beneficiary only if:

> (i) the person renders advice to the participant or beneficiary as to the value of securities or other property, or makes recommendations as to the advisability of investing in, purchasing, or selling securities or other property; and (ii) the person, either directly or indirectly, (A) has discretionary authority or control with respect to purchasing or selling securities or other property for the participant or beneficiary, or (B)

[94] Labor Department Interpretative Bulletin 96-1, 26 C.F.R. Sec. 2509.96.1.

> renders the advice on a regular basis to the participant or beneficiary, pursuant to a mutual agreement, arrangement or understanding (written or otherwise) with the participant or beneficiary that the advice will serve as a primary basis for the participant's or beneficiary's investment decisions with respect to plan assets and that such person will render individualized advice based on the particular needs of the participant or beneficiary.[95]

So, if the service provider meets one or either of these two criteria, the provider is providing investment advice and is subject to the fiduciary standard. But remember, whether particular investment-related information or materials provided to a participant or beneficiary constitutes the rendering of "investment advice" generally can only be determined by the facts and circumstances of the particular case with respect to the individual plan participant or beneficiary.

PPA Investment-Advice Fiduciary. Many plan sponsors have wanted to provide their employees with investment advice but, until the passage of PPA were concerned about the potential for fiduciary liability. PPA provides a way for advisers to 401(k) and 403(b) plans to provide investment advice without that advice becoming an act of self-dealing or a prohibited transaction. Two approaches may be taken. The first is under a structure whereby the advice provided has no impact on the level of compensation paid to the adviser. The second uses an automated and neutral model for making investment changes.

M. Mutual Fund Excessive Trading Policies

Mutual fund excessive trading policies place restrictions on participant trading of shares separate and apart from the plan imposed restrictions and participant directed account rules described in section D of this chapter. Mutual fund companies impose these policies to prevent market timing and day-trading participants adversely affect the performance of the fund. These adverse affects can include diluting share values, increasing fund transaction costs, interfering with the fund's portfolio management, and forcing funds to hold excess levels of cash in order to maintain sufficient liquidity to handle trading activity.

The policies often reserve the right to reject any trade or to limit round trip investing in a particular period. A "round trip" is described as a participant initiated exchange purchase followed by an exchange-redemption within the same

[95] Ibid.

fund within, for example, thirty days. One fund complex limits participants to one round trip transaction in a ninety-day rolling period.

N. An Alternative to Participant-Directed Investment Accounts

Participant-directed investment accounts have become such a dominant feature of 401(k) plans that some people believe the law requires them. This begs the question: "Why is this so?" The answer is both historical and marketing related. Current 401(k) arrangements grew out the individual retirement account platforms created by the financial industry and predating the arrival of 401(k) plans. The industry has done a very good job of selling this platform to plan sponsors. Often the key sales point is the protection from fiduciary liability participant directed accounts under ERISA section 404(c) provides (discussed in chapter 12). Whether that is in fact true is debatable, but whether it is or is not, this platform is strongly entrenched. An expensive apparatus of websites, daily valuation, participant education, and investment advice is built on this platform and there is contention about whether the system actually works in providing workers secure retirements.

Jeff Chang of the law firm of Chang Ruthenberg & Long PC has a common sense insight on this system—and a proposal.[96] He says:

"The likelihood of investment success *increases* as the participant's involvement in investment decisions *decreases*" [emphasis added].

And he cites studies that back him up. These studies have concluded:

- The more extensive or complicated a plan's menu of investment options, the more likely participants is to feel overloaded with choices and unable to invest their retirement accounts.[97]
- Participants who trade in their own accounts through so-called brokerage windows may suffer particularly poor investment performance due to higher transaction costs and greater risk of more active trading.[98]

[96] "A Step Beyond ERISA Section 404(c): Improving on the Participant Directed 401(k) Investment Model,"Chang Ruthenberg & Long PC website, http://www.seethebenefits.com/showarticle.aspx?Show=837.

[97] See Gur Huberman and Wei Jiang, "Offering vs. Choice in 401(k) Plans: Equity Exposure and Number of Funds" (working paper, Columbia Business School, September 2004 draft).

[98] See Terrance Odean, "Do Investors Trade Too Much?" *American Economic Review* 89 (December 1999): 1279–1298, http://faculty.haas.berkeley.edu/odean/Papers%20current%20versions/DoInvestors.pdf.

And according to a Tower Watson study that compared investment returns in defined-benefit plans and defined-contribution plans (such as 401[k] plans):

- Defined-benefit plans outperformed defined-contribution plans by an annual average of 76 basis points from 1995 to 2011, although this difference narrowed in later years.
- When stock market returns were poor, 2011 defined-benefit plans outperformed defined-contribution plans by 300 basis points.[99]

Chang suggests that plan sponsors consider a new model that achieves the two important goals that are not both being achieved under the participant-directed account approach:

- Increasing the chance that the retirement and investment needs of participants will be met
- Reducing the fiduciary responsibility (and liability) of plan fiduciaries

This model, which was *formerly* the standard model, and is called a "Non-Participant Directed Account 401(k) Plan." It would have the following features:

Plan sponsor responsibility:	Appoints investment manager such as RIA with full discretionary authority over all plan assets. Plan sponsor does not retain any investment authority. Qualifies and monitors performance of investment manager, including the following: 1. Evaluates investment manager's qualifications. 2. Ascertains the reasonableness of the investment manager's fees. 3. Carefully reviews documentation governing IM relationship.

99 http://www.towerswatson.com/en/Insights/Newsletters/Americas/Insider/2013/DB-Versus-DC-Investment-Returns-the-2009-2011-Update.

Asset allocation:	Subaccounts created reflecting appropriate asset allocations for various types of participants with different risk tolerances and investment time horizons.
Type of investments:	Low-cost, broadly diversified, and automatically rebalanced and passively managed mutual funds.
Investment manager responsibilities:	1. Creates and invests subaccounts according to the IPS it establishes. 2. Obtains information from participant (questionnaire/interview) to determine most appropriate portfolio for the participant. 3. Updates participant information periodically to determine whether portfolio continues to be appropriate.
Participant investment "responsibilities":	None. 1. Participants are *not responsible* for the investment in their accounts. 2. Participants cooperate with investment manager in providing information necessary to determine appropriate portfolio.

Plan sponsors and participants will benefit from this type of arrangement, in terms of protecting themselves from fiduciary liability, in two basic ways:

1. Plan sponsors are not be responsible for plan investment decisions or monitoring of plan options. These responsibilities will be the investment manager's, and so will the liability.
2. Plan sponsors do not have to comply with the 404(c) requirements, lifting the significant burden that comes with the proper application of those rules.
3. Plan participants will benefit from the professional management of their accounts that they would not otherwise have in a participant-directed account arrangement.

CHAPTER 13

Summary of Participant Disclosure Obligations

Federal rules relating to employee benefit plans are disclosure driven. The agencies believe that almost any problem be can cured with the disinfecting sunshine of the provision of lots of information to plan participants. Whether this approach has its intended effect is up for discussion. But be assured a plan sponsor that fails in its disclosure obligations will either lose valuable protections or be in violation of the law. This chapter describes the various disclosures that plan sponsors must make. Not all the disclosures are universally applicable. For example, a

SPD must be distributed by all plans. A quarterly participant account statement must be provided only to participants in plans allowing participants to direct investments in their accounts.

A. All Notices Summarized

Type of Notice	Description
Summary Plan Description (SPD) and Summary of Material Modifications (SMM)	The SPD is a plain-language summary of the plan it describes. The plan administrator is required to provide an SPD to employees after they join the plan and to beneficiaries after they first receive benefits. SPDs must be provided to participants and beneficiaries within thirty days of a request. SPDs must be restated once every five years. The SMM document describes changes to the plan or the SPD. The SMM or an updated SPD must be furnished automatically to participants within 210 days after the end of the plan year in which a change is adopted.
Summary Annual Report (SAR)	Must be provided to participants after the annual return for the plan is filed each year.
Quarterly Account Statement	Must be provided to participants who direct investments in their accounts.
Qualified Default Investment Arrangement (QDIA) Notice	Must be provided to newly eligible employees and provided annually thereafter.
Eligible Automatic Contribution Arrangement (EACA) Notice	Must be provided to newly eligible employees and annually in plans that utilize EACA.
Qualified Automatic Contribution Arrangement (QACA)	Must be provided to newly eligible employees and annually in plans that utilize QACA.
Automatic Increase in Elective Deferrals	Must be provided annually in plans that incorporate automatic increase provisions.

Automatic Contribution Arrangement (ACA)	Must be provided to newly eligible employees and annually in plans that utilize ACA.
Safe Harbor Contributions Notice	Must be provided annually.
Fee and expense notices required under ERISA section 404(a)(5)	See section B, below.
Plan Document	Must be provided within thirty days of request to a plan participant or beneficiary.

POINTER: The plan sponsor should designate someone that will be directly responsible for delivering these notices or for overseeing the service providers that have been delegated the responsibility.

B. ERISA Section 404(a)(5) Notice Requirements

According to the Labor Department, ERISA section 404(a)(5) notices are intended to give participants access to the information they need to make informed decisions, including information about fees and expenses. The information provided in the annual notices falls into three basic categories:

- **Plan-related information**, including information about the structure and mechanics of the plan; an explanation of how to give investment instructions under the plan; a current list of the plan's investment options and a description of any "brokerage windows" or similar arrangement that enables the selection of investments beyond those designated by the plan; administrative expense information; and individual expense information.
- **Investment-related information**, including performance data, benchmarking information, fee and expense information, website information, and a glossary of investment terms.
- **Fee-related information** in quarterly statements showing the deduction of fees and expenses.

POINTER: Responsibility for the delivery of these disclosures lies with the plan administrator, although in many cases responsibility for the delivery will be assigned to the plan service provider. Plan sponsors must review these disclosures for completeness and accuracy and oversee their delivery.

CHAPTER 14

Reporting to the Labor Department

The Labor Department (and the IRS) wants to know what is going on with your plan and it wants plan participants to know too. Consequently, plan sponsors are required to file annual information returns, report if a service provider has not made a required fee disclosure, and report tax information to the IRS. This chapter describes these basic reporting obligations.

A. Annual Information Return (Form 5500 Series)

Plan administrators (usually the plan sponsor) are required to file, under penalty of perjury, annual information returns with the Labor Department. Form 5500 and related schedules provide information to the Labor Department that it uses in its administration of ERISA and particularly in identifying plans for examination. The IRS also use return information is also used by to target plans under its examination program.

Each annual return is a matter of public record and is available for all to see at the Labor Department website (https://www.efast.dol.gov/portal/app/disseminate?execution=e1s1).

In general, the report elicits information on participation, service provider fees, plan assets, prohibited transactions, and other aspects of plan administration. An independent accountant must do a financial audit of plans with more than a hundred participants audited and their report submitted with the return.

The Labor Department is asking plan sponsors subject to ERISA to pay closer attention to fee transparency and to whether plan sponsors are obtaining the information necessary to assess the compensation relative to services provided. A large plan (one hundred participants or more) must report on Schedule C the *direct* or *indirect* compensation paid to service providers on the following basis:

- All service providers who received compensation of $5,000 or more
- The relationship of that service provider to the plan sponsor
- The total amount of direct compensation paid

For purposes of this reporting:

- *Direct compensation* is compensation a service provider receives directly from the plan. For example, payments by the plan to a third-party vendor for record-keeping services are considered direct compensation. However, payments by the plan sponsor for services provided to the plan and not reimbursed by the plan are not subject to Schedule C reporting.
- *Indirect compensation* is compensation a service provider receives from sources other than the plan or plan sponsor if the compensation was received in connection with services rendered to the plan. For example, it includes fees or expense-reimbursement payments charged to investment funds and reflected in the value of the investment or return on investment of the participating plan or its participants, finders' fees, "soft dollar" revenue, float revenue, and/or brokerage commissions or other transaction-based fees for transactions or services involving the plan that were not paid directly by the plan sponsor.

The plan administrator must electronically deliver the return to the Labor Department no later than the end of the last day of the seventh month following the end of the plan year for which the return is required. For example, a plan whose year ends on December 31 has until July 31 of the year following to file the return. An automatic one-and-a-half-month extension is provided to plans whose plan years are the same as the employer's tax year and the employer has filed an extension of its tax return. An additional two-and-a-half-month extension of the normal seven-month filing period is available by timely filing a Form 5558.

EFAST2 is the all-electronic system used by plan administrators for the submission, receipt, and processing of the Form 5500 series forms. Under EFAST2, filers choose between using EFAST2-approved vendor software or the Labor Department website (IFILE) to prepare and submit Form 5500 or Form 5500-SF. Completed forms are submitted via the Internet to EFAST2 for processing.

POINTER: The TPA generally prepares the return for the signature of the plan administrator and the timely delivery of the return to the Labor Department. The review of the return cannot be a rubber stamp, and it is important for the plan administrator to have a draft of the report well before the filing date so the review is careful and issues are addressed. The TPA may not have direct information about some aspects of the form that only the plan administrator or plan sponsor will know.

POINTER: I have noticed that sometimes there is confusion about the appropriate signatory for these returns. The plan sponsor is often the "plan administrator" designated in plan documents, yet plan sponsor staff will sign the return as plan administrator. The better approach in that case is to sign the form in something like the following fashion: "XYZ Widget Company by Sally Jones, Director of Human Resources."

Penalties for filing failures. The Labor Department and IRS can assess various per-day penalties, up to a maximum, for filing failures. Filing failures include the delinquent or incomplete filing of a return. Penalties can range from $25 to $300 per day, up to a maximum of $50,000.

The Labor Department has a Delinquent Filer Voluntary Compliance Program (DFVCP), discussed in chapter 15, that provides penalty relief for some of these filing failures.

B. Failure of Covered Service Provider to Provide Fee Disclosures

If a covered service provider fails to provide a disclosure of its fees and other information, as described in chapter 7, the responsible plan fiduciary must notify the Labor Department of the failure using a form provided by the department (Fee Disclosure Failure Notice). The notice can be filed online or by visiting the Labor Department website (http://askebsa.dol.gov/fdfn/).

If the responsible plan fiduciary does not receive a required disclosure or if, on review of the submitted material, discovers that a covered service provider failed to disclose all of the required information, the fiduciary must request the missing information in writing. A covered service provider has ninety days to provide the proper disclosures. When a service provider refuses to provide the disclosures or does not respond within ninety days, the plan sponsor must notify the Labor Department.[100]It must also fire the service provider or as the rule says terminate the contract for future services "as expeditiously as possible."

[100] Within thirty days of the earlier of the refusal to provide information or the expiration of the ninety-day window.

C. Income Tax Reporting and Withholding

This book does not cover tax reporting and withholding, but you should remember that payments made from a plan are subject to income tax withholding and reporting. Procedures should be established to ensure that withholding, remittance of withholding to the IRS, and reporting of that withholding are all accomplished as required by the Internal Revenue Code.

CHAPTER 15

Enforcement and Broken Plan Correction Programs

There is no employee benefit plan that does not during the course of its existence run into problems that must be fixed. Some problems can be resolved without government involvement. For others there is no other choice but to use a government fix-it programs. This chapter describes those, sometimes quite forgiving, programs. In general, these programs reduce substantially the potentially high tax, penalty and other costs associated with plan mistakes.

A. Agency Enforcement

Four government agencies are responsible for the regulation of pension and benefit plan activities: the (1) Labor Department, (2) IRS, (3) Securities and Exchange Commission (SEC), and (4) Pension Benefit Guaranty Corporation (PBGC). The SEC rules are beyond the scope of this book, and the PBGC does not have jurisdictional oversight over the types of pension plans discussed in this book. We can safely ignore them in this book.

Labor Department. The Employee Benefits Security Administration (EBSA) of this agency is primarily responsible for administering the fiduciary responsibility provisions of ERISA. Its rules describe requirements for the conduct of individuals and entities that are plan fiduciaries and service providers and for the reporting and disclosure of plan information to plan participants, beneficiaries, and EBSA. EBSA is responsible for ensuring the integrity of the private employee-benefit plan system in the United States. EBSA's oversight authority extends to nearly 684,000 retirement plans, 24 million health plans, and a similar number of other welfare benefit plans, such as those providing life or disability insurance.

In fiscal year 2013, EBSA closed 3,677 civil investigations, with 2,677 (72.8 percent) resulting in monetary results for plans or other corrective action. Nationwide in fiscal year 2013, EBSA also referred 190 matters for civil litigation. EBSA also closed 320 criminal investigations, which led to the indictment of 88 individuals—including plan officials, corporate officers, and service providers—for offenses related to employee-benefit plans. For the most part, the failure to comply with ERISA is not willful.

Currently, EBSA has the following national enforcement programs:

- Contributory Plans Criminal Project
- Rapid ERISA Action Team
- Employee Stock Ownership Plans (ESOPs)
- Consultant/Adviser Project (focus is on improper or undisclosed compensation)
- Desk Reviews of Form 5500
- Work Paper Audits

IRS. The IRS has jurisdiction over employee-benefit plans under the provisions of the Internal Revenue Code governing qualified plans such as 401(k) plans, 403(b) plans, 457 governmental plans, and welfare benefit plans. IRS sanctions for noncompliance can be quite severe including loss of deductions for contributions to the plan, taxation of trust earnings, and taxation of participants. The IRS has an active plan examination program.

B. Employee Plans Compliance Resolution System

The Employee Plans Compliance Resolution System (EPCRS)[101] is an IRS program that allows plan sponsors to avoid plan disqualification by correcting plan compliance failures and to continue providing their employees with retirement benefits on a tax-favored basis.[102] The components of the EPCRS program provide for self-correction of plan failures, voluntary correction with IRS approval, and correction on audit.

---

[101] Revenue Procedure 2013-12, 2013-04 I.R.B. 313.

[102] Plan disqualification results in a loss of deductions for contributions made to the plan for "for profit" entities and the taxation of trust earnings and current taxation of participants for both tax-exempt and for-profit employers.

The Self-Correction Program (SCP) allows a plan sponsor that has *established compliance practices and procedures* to correct certain insignificant plan failures at any time and certain significant failures within two years without payment, fee, or sanction.

The Voluntary Correction Program (VCP) permits a plan sponsor to make corrections with IRS approval any time before an audit and to pay a limited fee.

Commonly corrected errors under this program include the following failures:[103]

- Timely update plan
- Follow the terms of plan
- Follow plan definition of compensation for purpose of determining contributions
- Make contributions to all eligible employees
- Average Deferral Percentage and Average Contribution Percentage testing
- Give eligible employees an opportunity to make salary deferrals
- Follow hardship distribution rules
- Make top-heavy contributions
- Distribute summary annual report
- Timely deposit of elective deferrals
- Distribution of excess deferrals
- Follow required minimum distribution rules

POINTER: Maintaining a calendar to schedule each of these areas of vulnerability will either nip problems in the bud or prevent them from becoming costly to fix.

The Audit Closing Agreement Program (Audit CAP) allows plan failures that are discovered on audit to be corrected, but the sponsor must pay a sanction that is related to the severity of the failure, taking into account the extent of any correction made before the audit.

C. Voluntary Fiduciary Correction Program

The Labor Department's Voluntary Fiduciary Correction (VFC) Program encourages remedial compliance efforts by parties that have engaged in certain violations of the fiduciary rules covering qualified plans and 403(b) plans. To be eligible to participate in the program, a fiduciary may not currently be under investigation by the Labor Department.

[103] See IRS, "401(k) Fix-It Guide," http://www.irs.gov/pub/irs-tege/401k_mistakes.pdf.

Examples of transactions that are eligible for the VFC Program include delinquent participant contributions to pension plans, loans with parties-in-interest, and benefit payments based on improper valuation of plan assets.

D. Delinquent Filer Voluntary Compliance Program

Plan fiduciaries that engage in prohibited transactions may be able to avoid excise taxes and other penalties through a filing under the Delinquent Filer Voluntary Compliance Program (DFVCP). The Labor Department will consider an application if the applicant is not considered "under investigation" and the violation is for a transaction described in the Labor Department's procedures. As a condition for this relief, applicants have to make the plan whole and may have to notify plan participants of the violation.

POINTER: The DFVCP is quite forgiving and can greatly reduce exposures to penalties for filing failures that have stretched out over a number of years.

CHAPTER 16

Alternative and Next Generation Plan Management: Approaches to Plan Administration and Controlling Fiduciary Liability

The world is changing and where it might go in terms of benefit plan service models is anyone's guess. Yet there are some trends and new ideas that are very much worth watching and perhaps adopting. This chapter discusses those developments.

A. Accelerating Burdens of Plan Sponsorship

For large plan sponsors, the tasks associated with running a 401(k) plan are daunting. For smaller employers, the burden is even worse because of fewer available human and financial resources. These tasks or responsibilities include, as described earlier in this book:

- Administrative compliance
- Legal compliance
- Investments
- Selection and monitoring of service providers
- Participant communications and required disclosures

All of this involves staff time, increased overhead, and dealings with multiple service providers that include advisors, agents, brokers, attorneys, accountants, TPAs, trustees, investment managers, and others. And ERISA measures the plan sponsor's conduct against the standard of a prudent expert, with personal and corporate liability the price of failure. When one considers the increased attention both the IRS and Labor Department are giving plan sponsor management and controls and the demand put on employers to evaluate and monitor service providers, it is small wonder that employers of all sizes are looking for ways to shift their responsibilities to those who are experts and truly capable of handling those responsibilities.

B. Traditional Outsourcing

In a limited sense, the shifting of responsibility to those who have the proficiency to do the work has been going on for years through traditional outsourcing. Plan sponsors do not currently handle plan record keeping and investment execution (buy/sell). Most do not produce their own plan documents, and many outsource plan testing to non-fiduciary administrators. More "accountable" plan administration is available under ERISA section 3(16) plan administrators, but to date, these types of arrangements have not been common. Similarly responsibility for plan investment decisions may be shifted to 3(38) investment managers. Responsibility for poor individual investment decisions can be shifted to plan participants via the ERISA section 404(c) election.

Broker and investment company representations, however, often provide the illusion of shifting fiduciary responsibilities from plan sponsors without actually doing so. Often plan sponsors do not understand this, due to ambiguous service provider representations or claims concerning the extent of the fiduciary services they offer. It does not help that many of the words used seem to mean the same thing but actually have important and distinct legal meanings. For example, the words "recordkeeper," "third-party administrator," and "plan administrator" appear to mean the same thing, but only a "plan administrator" is a plan fiduciary under ERISA.

Similarly, these brokers and investment companies will claim that they are investment fiduciaries but will so severely limit what they are responsible for as fiduciaries that the status itself does not protect the plan sponsor one iota. In other words, plan sponsors continue to retain just as much fiduciary responsibility and associated liability after hiring these service providers as they had before. Despite the claims in provider brochures, the shifting of responsibility to these providers is by no means complete under applicable statutory and regulatory rules and as a matter of risk protection to the plan sponsor.

C. Historical Efforts for More Complete Outsourcing

Historically plan sponsors have desired freedom from retirement plan management responsibility. The marketplace has responded with multiple arrangements to shift the plan management and fiduciary responsibility burden. Each arrangement has intended advantages and downside issues.

Some plan sponsors have looked to shift not just the plan management burden, but also the entire employer/employee relationship burden to professional employer organizations (PEOs). These entities manage the entire employment relationship administrative burden from payroll to health insurance and employee benefits. Others have joined so-called open MEPs, or multiple-employer plans, under which only the burden of managing the administration of 401(k) plan benefits is shifted—to an independent entity with expertise in the management of plans. Others, as explained above, have incompletely or partially shifted these responsibilities, with the attendant limitations that type of arrangement has, as described above.

There is a new arrangement coming into the marketplace, as a response to both the historic burdens of plan sponsorship and to a regulatory environment that increasingly forces plan sponsors to be ERISA experts.[104] It allows plan sponsors to keep the unique investment and plan management features of their existing plans while shifting entirely the management burden—including most of the fiduciary risk—to an independent expert plan management entity. These arrangements are called "professional administrator plan arrangements"(PAPAs). They shift responsibility without some of the drawbacks of the other arrangements.

Let's look at each of these arrangements in more detail.

D. Professional Employer Organizations

Under a PEO, an employer essentially outsources their employees through a joint or "co-employment" relationship with the PEO. Management tasks, such as employee benefits, payroll, and workers' compensation; recruiting; risk/safety management; and training and development are handled by an independent entity. The PEO does this by hiring a client company's employees, thus becoming their employer of record for tax and insurance purposes.

Intended advantages: PEOs bring value to businesses by allowing them to outsource business processes related to payroll and tax compliance, human resources, employee benefits, and workers' compensation, thereby freeing them up to engage in their primary business activities. PEOs normally offer 401(k) and

[104] Witness the burdens placed on employers in connection with the evaluation of service provider disclosures under DOL's new service provider disclosure rules.

other benefit plans to their "co-employees." So, as a consequence of the arrangement, the PEO handles the management and administration of the 401(k) plan and is the responsible of fiduciary for the plan. Client-employers are not responsible in any sense, fiduciary or otherwise, for a PEO plan.

Potential disadvantages: Unless there is a good business case for using the PEO—apart from the advantages of shifting 401(k) sponsorship responsibilities—there is no reason to utilize this arrangement.

E. Open Multiple-Employer Plans

A consulting firm typically sponsors an open MEP for more than one employer that lack any connection or relationship to one another. The sponsoring entity purports to assume the bulk of the fiduciary responsibility for the operations and investments of the plan, including the hiring and supervision of plan service providers.

Intended advantages: Open MEPs shift management and fiduciary burdens to a professional entity or administrator. They can also offer economies of scale for administration and investments.

Disadvantages: Labor Department advisory opinions call into question these arrangements. There are also disadvantages under the Internal Revenue Code including the possibility that the entire plan can be tax-disqualified based on the actions of one "bad-apple" participating employer, affecting all employers who participate in the plan.

These plans can be a bit difficult to get out of when a plan decides to terminate the plan or set up its own individual plan. Generally speaking a participants service with any one participating employer of the plan counts as service with other participating employers. This means that if an employee terminates employment with a participating employer for employment with another participating employer his service for eligibility, vesting and benefit accrual purposes will be carried over to the new employer.

Since the issuance of the Labor Department advisory opinions, most open MEP arrangements that clearly do not satisfy the Labor Department-required commonality standard have either ceased operations entirely or have modified their operations to take the new guidance into account. Those that have revised their operations typically continue to administer the program as if it were a single plan, but they prepare separate Form 5500s and separate audits and purchase separate fidelity bonds for each participating employer group. Many of these arrangements now also calculate plan expense charges based solely on the asset levels of each separate plan, instead of aggregating the assets of all participating plans together to obtain lower expense ratios (on a larger pot of money).

In sum, open MEPs have lost the advantages of MEP status under Labor Department rules, while they continue to be regarded as MEPs under IRS rules—which means they continue to be burdened with all the Internal Revenue Code limitations described above, which have always been attendant on them.[105]

F. Professional Administrator Plan Arrangements

The professional administrator plan arrangement or PAPA is an exciting new development among the trends in the 401(k)/403(b) industry today. Under a PAPA, all plan management responsibilities normally associated with plan sponsorship are transferred to a professional, independent plan administrator (IPA) who is a "plan administrator" and "fiduciary," as those terms are defined in ERISA, and who agrees to be an ERISA named fiduciary and to take on complete discretionary investment authority with respect to the investment of plan assets. Under the arrangement the plan sponsor can off-load many important and time consuming responsibilities to a professional who will assume almost all of the plan sponsor's fiduciary responsibility for the plan.

The advantages and disadvantages of the PAPA are summarized below.

Advantages: All plan management responsibilities and almost all fiduciary responsibilities end for the plan sponsor. Once the transfer is complete, the IPA has fiduciary responsibility in each of the following areas:

- Administrative compliance
- Legal compliance
- Investments
- Participant education
- Selection and monitoring of service providers
- Participant communications and required disclosures

The plan sponsor is no longer responsible for, or has fiduciary liability with respect to, managing plan service providers, overseeing plan investments, or preparing and filing annual returns on Form 5500. For some plan sponsors, hundreds of hours of staff time can be saved.

Disadvantages are limited in a PAPA: The sponsor remains responsible, as any plan sponsor would, for the initial selection and monitoring of the performance

[105] The discussion in this section is taken almost verbatim from "A Multiple Employer Plans (MEPs) Primer" presented to the American Tax Association Section of Taxation 2013 September Meeting; San Francisco, California, Tax Meeting; Friday, September 20, 2013; by Carol L. Myers, Esq., of Sarasota, Florida, and Charles G. Humphrey, Esq., of Andover, Massachusetts.

of the IPA and for reviewing reports the IPA provides concerning administration of the plan. This is the irreducible minimum of fiduciary responsibility required of plan sponsors under ERISA. This is not a disadvantage that is unique to a PAPA. In fact, there is no plan sponsor that can ever rid itself of this responsibility.

PAPAs may be inevitable for many employers in today's regulatory environment, and my expectation is that they will become more common. Plan sponsors do not want the burden of plan management and do not want to be experts, as the Labor Department requires them to be. Yet they want plan arrangements that are specifically tailored to their own needs. PAPAs uniquely solve these problems for employers and are a potentially priceless tool for plan sponsors.

G. What to Look for in a PAPA

Opting to use a professional administrator plan arrangement, or PAPA, and selecting an IPA are subject to the normal prudence requirements present in the selection of any other service provider. These are, among others, the important considerations:

- What are the IPA's reputation, expertise, and financial soundness?
- Is the IPA committing to be the named fiduciary, plan administrator, and investment fiduciary?
- Does the IPA promise broad services and protection in its sales materials and weaseling out of its "promises" in the contracts it wants the plan sponsor to sign?
- Is the IPA receiving payments from other plan service providers in connection with services to the plan (revenue sharing or "pay to play")?
- Does it maintain recognized prudent processes and procedures?
- Does the IPA maintain adequate insurance coverage and bonding?
- Is the IPA adequately staffed, and does it provide its staff and other key players with annual fiduciary and regulatory updates and training?
- Is the IPA certified annually by a professional certification entity such as CEFEX?[106]
- Is it subject to any other examination or audits by regulatory authorities or others?
- Is the IPA's performance as to the plan reviewed by an independent expert who then provides a report to the plan sponsor?

[106] This certificaton is given to advisors who demonstrate adherence to the fiduciary best practices of this organization.

Terms Used in This Book

Annual return (Form 5500 series) is the informational return that plan administrators (read plan sponsors) *must* file with the Labor Department. It reports basic census data, plan assets, and service provider fees. Significant penalties can apply if the return is not filed on time. The IRS and the Labor Department often use this form as the basis for agency examinations and investigations.

Automatic Contribution Arrangement, or **ACA**, is an arrangement in a 401(k) or 403(b) plan that automatically reduces an employee's compensation by a fixed percentage and has the amount contributed to the employer's 401(k) plan. The default election ceases to apply if the employee makes an affirmative election.

Benchmarking is a process by which plan fees are compared to the fees paid by similar plans. Benchmarking results can be hugely disparate, depending on the sampling and assumptions used. An expert that is independent of the incumbent service provider should be used to run the benchmarking.

Broker-dealer is a person or firm in the business of buying and selling securities, operating as both a broker and a dealer, depending on the transaction. The term is used to describe stock brokerages. Many plan sponsors establish their plans using a broker-dealer.

Brokerage window is a feature under a 401(k) plan that allows participants to invest in individual stocks and securities rather than in the regular menu of mutual-fund investments. The participant's account is charged for this feature.

Bundled provider is a service provider, usually in the mutual-fund business, that supplies all key plan services, including custody of plan assets, record keeping, and third-party administrator services. The advantage to a plan sponsor that uses these services is that it only has to deal with one provider. The advantage to the mutual-fund company is that "the bundle" provides an easy-to-sell package for distribution of its mutual funds. Well-known names in the industry providing this service include American Funds and Fidelity, although there are many others.

Committee charter is a written document intended to guide the operation of committees that have plan investment or administration fiduciary responsibilities. Such a charter must be consistent with plan document provisions and can be highly useful in the effective and compliant administration of an employee-benefit plan.

Collective investment fund is a trust fund managed by a bank or trust company that pools assets from multiple plan sponsors in a manner similar to a mutual fund.

Covered service provider, or **CSP**, is a plan service provider that is required to disclose fee and service information, as specified in Labor Department regulations under section 2550.408b-2.

Custodian is a bank or trust company that holds assets for a plan. A custodian has no discretionary authority with regard to the investment of plan assets.

Delinquent Filer Voluntary Compliance Program, or **DFVCP**, is a Labor Department "forgiveness" program under which, and for a small fee, plan sponsors can file delinquent annual returns and avoid the much larger penalties that might otherwise apply.

Designated investment alternative, or **DIA**, is a term used to describe investments that have been selected by a plan sponsor or plan advisers for investment by participants in a plan that gives participants the right to direct investments.

Directors & Officers Insurance, or **D&O Insurance**, provides protection from personal liability for acts by directors and officers in those capacities. This insurance does not provide protection from their liability for their actions as ERISA fiduciaries, although riders can be purchased to provide this protection.

Eligible Automatic Contribution Arrangement, or **EACA**, is an arrangement in which participants are treated as having elected to defer an amount equal to a uniform percentage of compensation provided under the plan until they specifically opt out of the arrangement.

Employee Benefits Security Administration, or **EBSA**, is the agency within the Labor Department that administers the provisions of ERISA. It issues rules interpreting ERISA, grants prohibited transaction exemptions, and enforces the law through investigations, litigation, and other means.

Employee Plans Compliance Resolution System, or **EPCRS**, is the IRS plan correction program under which plan sponsors can correct errors relating to the administration of their plans that otherwise might lead to the loss of the tax benefits of a qualified plan, 403(b) plan, or SEP. It consists of three main parts: (1) SCP, or the Self-Correction Program; (2) VCP, or the Voluntary Correction Program; and (3) Audit CAP, or the Audit Closing Agreement Program.

ERISA, otherwise known as the **Employee Retirement Income Security Act of 1974**, is the federal law under which all plan sponsor activity as a fiduciary is measured. It also contains rules for reporting plan information to the government and for disclosing information to plan participants. ERISA is not without teeth, and it imposes various sanctions for fiduciary failures and prohibited transactions, including fines, excise taxes, and personal liability for plans losses.

ERISA fidelity bond is a bond required under section 512 of ERISA to protect a plan from theft, fraud, or dishonesty in the handling of plan funds. This bond should in no way be confused with providing plan fiduciaries ERISA fiduciary liability protection.

ERISA section 404(c) participant-directed account plan is a plan in which the plan sponsor intends to follow the rules of ERISA section 404(c) so that the plan sponsor will have greater protection from a claim by a participant that the plan sponsor has liability for a participant's investment decisions.

Employer real property is property owned by the plan and leased to the plan sponsor by a plan. The acquisition and leasing of the property is prohibited under the prohibited transaction rules unless the property qualifies as "qualifying real property" or is permitted under an individually granted exemption by the Labor Department. McDonalds, the hamburger people, at one time had many properties held by their plan(s) under the "qualifying real property" exemption and still may have.

Employer securities are the stock, debt obligation or partnership interest of a plan sponsor. A plan may nor acquire or hold employer securities unless they are "qualifying employer securities" as defined in ERISA.

Exchange traded fund, or **ETF**, is a security that tracks an index, a commodity, or an index fund and trades like a stock with prices that change throughout the trading day as shares are sold. Although these funds have experienced some plan sponsor interest, mutual fund investments are the dominant 401(k) investment.

Expense ratio is a fee charged as a percentage of assets to mutual fund investors. Typically these fees are between 0.20 percent and 2.0 percent of fund assets. The expense ratio consists of three categories of expense: investment management, administrative, and revenue sharing.

Fiduciary is a common- law term and a term specifically defined in ERISA. Under ERISA, the term includes as fiduciaries a plan administrator as defined in section 3(16); named fiduciaries as defined in section 402(a)(1); those who have discretionary responsibility for the administration of the plan and investment of plan assets; and investment-advice fiduciaries who provide advice regarding investments but do not make the ultimate decision to make a particular investment.

Fiduciary liability insurance or ERISA fiduciary liability insurance is insurance purchased to protect individuals in their activities as plan fiduciaries. This insurance should not be confused with directors and officer's insurance policies; the latter, without the purchase of a rider for this purpose, does not protect against claims of fiduciary liability. If an ERISA fiduciary liability policy is purchased with plan assets, insurance policy proceeds must to be paid to the plan, not to plan fiduciaries.

Fiduciary warranty or **guaranty** is a promise a service provider makes to a plan sponsor to assume fiduciary responsibility with respect to some aspect of the plan. The warranty or guarantee is typically given by the service provider to assure a plan sponsor that the provider is taking care of things by assuming fiduciary liability. In fact virtually all warranties are very limited and quite useless in providing real protections to plan sponsors. Read the contract not the sales literature and you will figure that out.

Float is money earned by financial institutions (such as banks and trust companies) on omnibus accounts the institution maintains to facilitate payments and disbursements from a plan. Typically, these accounts hold contributions and other assets pending investment directions from plan fiduciaries. For example, a plan fiduciary may direct the transfer of plan assets to a general account to make a distribution or other disbursement. During the time the amount is in the account and until the actual disbursement from the account, the financial institution retains earnings on the amount in the account. This is called "float." The Labor Department requires service providers to disclose float and for plan sponsors to consider whether the float plus the other fees paid the provider constitute reasonable compensation.

Hard-to-value investments are, as the term suggests, hard-to-value. Such investments may include limited partnership investments, employer securities, real property, personal property, and the like. These types of investments in plans provide special challenges to employers in terms of reporting plan asset values, understanding the true value of the investment, and making plan distributions.

Hedge fund is a limited partnership of investors that uses high-risk methods, such as investing with borrowed money, in hopes of realizing large capital gains.

Independent Qualified Plan Auditor Report, or **IQPA**, is required to be prepared and filed with the annual return (Form 5500) of plans with more than a hundred participants. The plan administrator is required to engage, on behalf of the plan participants, an independent qualified public accountant to examine the plan's financial statements. Any individual who, under state law, is licensed or certified to practice public accounting is eligible to be a "qualified public accountant" for this purpose, and the examination must be conducted in accordance with Generally Accepted Accounting Standards (GAAS). One of the purposes of this examination is to determine whether the plan's financial statements are presented in accordance with Generally Accepted Accounting Principles (GAAP).

Internal fiduciary or fiduciaries is the phrase used in this book to refer to ERISA fiduciaries who are the plan sponsor and its officers, employees, and board.

Internal Revenue Code, or **Code**, consists of rules that apply the tax laws to 401(k) and other deferred-compensation plans, such as 403(b) plans, 457 plans, and defined-benefit pension plans. Failure to comply with these rules can lead to the loss of the tax-favored status these plans have under the code. The Code also sets out rules for the taxation of benefits.

Investment adviser, as defined by the Investment Advisors Act of 1940, is any person or group that makes investment recommendations or conducts securities analysis in return for a fee, whether through direct management of client assets or via written publications.

Investment manager is a person or organization that makes investments in portfolios of securities on behalf of clients, in accordance with the investment objectives and parameters defined by these clients. An investment manager may be responsible for all activities associated with the management of client portfolios, from buying and selling securities on a day-to-day basis to portfolio monitoring, settlement of transactions, performance measurement, and regulatory and client reporting. An investment manager should not be confused with a "3(38) investment manager," as defined below.

Investment policy statement, or **IPS**, is "a written statement that provides the fiduciaries who are responsible for plan investments with guidelines or general instructions concerning various types or categories of investment management decisions" (from Labor Department Interpretive Bulletin 94-2). Federal law does not require investment policy statements, but they are an essential part of effectively run 401(k) plans.

Labor Department is the United States Department of Labor. This agency has jurisdiction over employee-benefit plans, including 401(k) and 403(b) plans. It exercises it authority primarily through the Employee Benefits Security Administration.

Multiple-employer plan, or **MEP**, is a retirement plan adopted by two or more employers who are unrelated for income tax purposes (that is, not members of a controlled group or other related groups under the Internal Revenue Code).

Mutual fund *is* an investment vehicle made up of a pool of funds collected from many investors for the purpose of investing in securities such as stocks, bonds, money-market instruments, and similar assets. A mutual fund's portfolio is structured and maintained to match the investment objectives stated in its prospectus. The fund's managers must invest in accordance with the fund's investment objectives.

Named fiduciary is an individual or entity required by law to be identified in the plan document that has discretionary responsibility for the administration of the plan or the investment of plan assets.

Open-source architecture is a format that allows plans to select investments from hundreds of mutual funds without impacting a provider's fees to the plan.

Participant-directed account is an account maintained for a participant in a defined-contribution plan, such as a 401(k) plan. The participant has the right to direct the investment of the account's funds, usually from a menu of investments selected by the plan sponsor or its advisers or investment managers.

Plan administrator, or "**3(16) plan administrator**," is the plan sponsor unless someone else is designated in the plan document or is appointed to the position. A plan administrator is a fiduciary. This position should not be confused with a recordkeeper or third-party administrator, who are not generally fiduciaries and who have different responsibilities.

Plan asset is an asset owned by the plan. The concept is not as straightforward as it seems. For example, salary-deferral contributions that are not transferred from plan sponsor to the plan are plan assets, even though they are not yet in the possession of the plan. Sometimes the underlying assets of a plan investment such as a limited partnership are plan assets. The concept has important implications for the application of the general fiduciary and prohibited-transaction rules.

Plan sponsor is a term used in this book to refer to the employer who adopts and maintains a plan for the benefit of its employees.

PAPA, or **professional administrator plan arrangement**, is an arrangement under which a plan sponsor can off-load nearly all plan administrative and fiduciary responsibilities to a professional administrator.

Professional employer organization, or **PEO**, is a firm that provides a service under which an employer can outsource employee management tasks, such as employee benefits, payroll and workers' compensation, recruiting, risk/safety management, and training and development. It does this by hiring a client company's employees and becoming their employer of record for tax and insurance purposes. PEOs often maintain 401(k) and other plan benefits for these employees. For purposes of the 401(k) plan, the IRS considers the employee to be an employee of the employer, not the PEO.

Prohibited transaction is a transaction involving a person related to the plan (called a party in interest or disqualified person) that is forbidden under federal law. For example, a plan may not loan funds to a plan sponsor. Acts of self-dealing by plan fiduciaries are also forbidden. Prohibited transactions are subject to sanction under the IRS and provisions of ERISA. Certain transactions are exempt under specific rules set forth in ERISA or in administrative exemptions granted by the Labor Department.

Qualified Automatic Contribution Arrangement, or **QACA**, is an arrangement under a 401(k) plan where each eligible employee is automatically enrolled in the plan at a specified salary deferral contribution rate.

Qualified Default Investment Arrangement, or **QDIA**, is an optional feature in a participant-directed investment 401(k) plan through which a participant who does not elect an investment option is automatically defaulted into an investment option chosen by the plan sponsor.

Recordkeeper is a service provider that keeps track of amounts in 401(k) plan accounts: how much is invested and earned, including the different types of contributions in a 401(k) plan that must be tracked—for example, salary deferral, employer matching, employer profit sharing, qualified non-elective contributions, and rollover. Recordkeepers may also perform other services, such as maintaining a participant website for account information and transfers, printing and mailing account statements to employees, requesting trades and other transactions within participant accounts, providing retirement calculators and guidance, producing enrollment and education materials, and maintaining toll-free customer service lines for plan participants.

Request for information, or **RFI**, is an informal process usually conducted by a consultant for a plan sponsor in which the consultant requests fee quotes from potential plan service providers "on a no-names" basis. The intention of the RFI is to make a determination of whether there is a real opportunity for reducing fees by considering other providers. The RFI is generally a better determinant than a benchmarking and is quite often followed by an RFP.

Request for proposal, or **RFP**, is a formal process usually conducted by a consultant in which the consultant asks potential service providers for firm fee quotes based on specific information about the plan with identification of the plan sponsor.

Revenue sharing refers to several different types of fees relating to mutual fund investments. These are 12b-1 fees, subtransfer agent fees, shareholder servicing fees, and profit-sharing payments. Sometimes these fees are referred to as "hidden fees" because they may be paid to plan service providers indirectly. Service providers are required to disclose these fees to plan sponsors, and plan sponsors are required to determine whether any revenue sharing paid to providers is reasonable compensation.

Section 3(38) investment manager. Under ERISA section 3(38), an investment manager is an individual or entity that takes discretion, authority, and/or control over the investment of a plan's assets and is one of the following: (a) a bank, (b) an insurance company, or (c) a registered investment adviser. ERISA provides that a plan sponsor can delegate to the 3(38) investment manager fiduciary the significant responsibility (and significant liability) of selecting, monitoring, and replacing investments. Delegation to such an investment manager, as defined under ERISA, relieves the plan sponsor of liability under ERISA for the individual investment decisions of the manager.

Self-Correction Program, or **SCP**, is a program under the IRS Employee Plans Compliance Resolution System (EPCRS) that allows plan sponsors to correct problems relating to the operation of their plans without penalty and without notification to the IRS.

Settlor expenses are expenses of the plan sponsor that may never be paid from plan assets. Examples are payments to consultants for plan design work and any other expense that is not related to the administration of a plan.

Share class is a designation for mutual-fund shares. The classes indicate the type and number of fees charged for the shares in a fund. A mutual fund may have as many as seven or more classes of shares for a particular fund, although in practice the types of share classes offered to 401(k) and 403(b) plans are limited.

Soft dollars are revenue paid to brokerages under Securities Exchange Commission (SEC) rule 28(e). For example, a mutual fund may offer to pay for research from a brokerage firm by executing trades at the brokerage.

Subtransfer agent, or **sub-TA fees**, are fees paid by trust companies, banks, and mutual-fund companies to subcontractors to track buy and sell orders and credit them to appropriate accounts.

Summary annual report, or **SAR**, is a report the plan administrator must provide to participants each year summarizing pertinent information in a plan's annual return (Form 5500 series).

Summary of material modifications, or **SMM**, is a document that can be used to supplement and/or be used instead of an SPD when a change is made in the plan that would otherwise be described in the SPD.

Summary plan description, or **SPD**, is a document that the plan administrator must provide to participants when they become eligible to participate in a plan. The SPD is intended to briefly describe important provisions of the plan and gives participants notice of their rights under ERISA.

Third-party administrator, or **TPA**, is the plan service provider responsible for day-to-day administration of the plan, including discrimination testing, distributions, preparing annual information returns and other government forms, and asset reconciliation.

Trustee is a bank, trust company, or individual who holds plan assets for investment. Trustee responsibilities are highly variable. Some may have complete discretionary authority for plan investments, and others may be directed by a plan committee and have no discretionary authority over investments.

12b-1 fees are fees that are included as part of a mutual fund's expense ratio and used to pay for sales commissions or account servicing or to offset the cost of plan services.

Unbundled provider arrangement is a service provider arrangement that allows plan sponsors to choose among a variety of recordkeeper, custodian, and education providers. The plan or the plan sponsor is billed separately for administrative and other services such as TPA and investment advice.

Voluntary Correction Program, or **VCP**, is a program under the IRS Employee Plans Compliance Resolution System (EPCRS) that allows plan sponsors to voluntarily fix problems with their plans without sanction or the necessity of involving the IRS in the correction. Use of the program can significantly reduce professional fees because there is no need to seek IRS approval.

Voluntary Fiduciary Correction Program, or VFCP, is a Labor Department "forgiveness" program that permits plan sponsors to correct prohibited transactions with potentially significantly reduced fines and penalties. Use of the program requires application to the Labor Department and approval.

Conclusion

In my thirty-five plus years as an ERISA and benefits attorney, I have found that effective plans are not effective by happenstance: one person cannot do it all in this highly specialized area and that plans do not run effectively and compliantly unless the right talents are brought to the table. These talents are investment advisory, investment management, administrative, accounting and legal to name a few. *A team makes **all** the difference.* In addition, there is always a strong leadership commitment to doing things right and this commitment is clearly communicated to the team and to others. I hope this book will serve as a resource that those who have that leadership commitment can use to organize their teams to achieve secure retirements for their participants.

Finally, for those of you who have read the entire book, thank you. ERISA fiduciary responsibility is not the most stimulating of topics, even in a book that is intended to cut through the jargon. For those of you who are using the book as a reference source I trust that you have found the organization of the book conducive to finding and understanding the issues that are important to you. For all of you whom this book has helped in adopting or further enhancing your fiduciary responsibility ethos, welcome to the way plan management should be!

Regardless of the type of reader you are, I want to have your thoughts: ideas for improvements, topics, or areas you think I have missed or should have explained more thoroughly are all are welcome. Give me a call at 716-465-7505 or email me at chumphrey@fiduciaryplangovernance.com. You now know where to find me and I hope you do.

Index

About the Author

Charles G. Humphrey, Esq.
Benefits & ERISA Counsel, Fiduciary Plan Governance, LLC

Chuck Humphrey has concentrated his practice in the area of ERISA and employee-benefits law for over thirty-five years, assisting corporate and tax-exempt employers with their benefit-plan obligations and financial institutions with their retirement-plan product offerings.

He is an original member of the IRS Northeast Pension Liaison Committee; a vice chair of the American Bar Association (ABA) Subcommittee on Multiple Employer, Professional Employer Organizations, and Controlled and Affiliated Service Groups; and a member of the Fiduciary Responsibility/ Plan Investments Subcommittee of the ABA. He is also a member of the New England Employee Benefits Council, where he is on the planning committees for the NEEBC's two major annual events, the Benefits Fair and Trade Show and the Washington Update. He is a former member the IRS National Determination Letter Committee.

Mr. Humphrey speaks and writes frequently on topics related to employee-benefit plans. He holds an undergraduate degree in history from the University of Michigan and a law degree from the University of Buffalo Law School. He is admitted to practice in New York and Washington, DC.

When he is not "fiduciating," Chuck can be found on the local ski hills, charging the net on a tennis court, or running his MINI Cooper at the track.

30023763R00095

Made in the USA
Charleston, SC
01 June 2014